New Impressions of Africa

Nouvelles Impressions d'Afrique

ƎƆAҀ ⅁ИIƆAℲ FACING PAGES

NICHOLAS JENKINS
Series Editor

New Impressions of Africa

Nouvelles Impressions d'Afrique

RAYMOND ROUSSEL

ILLUSTRATIONS BY HENRI-A. ZO

Translated with an introduction and notes by Mark Ford

PRINCETON UNIVERSITY PRESS
Princeton & Oxford

Copyright © 2011 by Princeton University Press

Published by Princeton University Press, 41 William Street,
Princeton, New Jersey 08540

In the United Kingdom: Princeton University Press, 6 Oxford
Street, Woodstock, Oxfordshire OX20 1TW

press.princeton.edu

Second printing, and first paperback printing, 2013
Paperback ISBN 978-0-691-15603-3

The Library of Congress has cataloged the cloth edition of this book
as follows

Roussel, Raymond, 1877–1933.
  [Nouvelles impressions d'Afrique. English & French]
  New impressions of Africa = Nouvelles impressions d'Afrique /
Raymond Roussel ; translated with an introduction and notes
by Mark Ford.
    p. cm. — (Facing pages)
  French with English translation on facing pages.
  ISBN 978-0-691-14459-7 (cloth : alk. paper)
  I. Ford, Mark, 1962 June 24- II. Title. III. Title: Nouvelles
impressions d'Afrique.
  PQ2635.O96168N613 2011
  841′.912—dc22   2010035414

British Library Cataloging-in-Publication Data is available

This book has been composed in Adobe Garamond

Printed on acid-free paper. ∞

Printed in the United States of America

10 9 8 7 6 5 4 3 2

this translation

is dedicated to

John Ashbery

Contents

Introduction

Nouvelles Impressions d'Afrique is the last work that the French poet, playwright, and novelist Raymond Roussel published during his lifetime. He began drafting it in 1915, but the poem was not to appear until the autumn of 1932, less than a year before its author was found dead in his room at the Grande Albergo e delle Palme in Palermo, Sicily at the age of 56. "*On ne saurait croire,*" he observed in his posthumously published essay, "Comment j'ai écrit certains de mes livres," "*quel temps immense exige la composition de vers de ce genre*" ("It is hard to believe the immense amount of time composition of this kind of verse requires").

The poem consists of four cantos of 228, 642, 172, and 232 lines respectively. Each is prefaced by a heading referring to a location in Egypt, and each begins with a few lines evoking the location in question. "*Rasant le Nil,*" opens Canto IV, which presents, initially at least, the Gardens of Rosetta as seen from a *dahabieh* (an Egyptian houseboat): "*je vois fuir deux rives couvertes / De fleurs, d'ailes, d'éclairs, de riches plantes vertes*" ("Skimming the Nile, I see flitting by two banks covered / With flowers, with wings, with flashes of brightness, with rich green plants"). The notion, however, that the poem will offer the reader a prettily versified travelogue is fast disrupted by the appearance of a bracket introducing a parenthetical thought, and soon after that, this parenthetical thought is itself interrupted by another bracket launching a second divagation, which is then itself interrupted by a third bracket and a new stream of related observations that are in turn interrupted by a fourth bracket, with its new line of discourse . . . Roussel also makes use of footnotes that may themselves contain as many as three sets of

1

brackets, removing us yet further from the canto's opening lines of description or meditation.

Each canto is, thus, grammatically, one enormously long sentence, and to complete its opening syntactic unit you have to turn forward to the lines that succeed the canto's final closing bracket. Canto IV, for instance, continues from the third line, "*Dont une suffirait à vingt de nos salons*" ("Of which one [rich green plant] could provide twenty of our salons") . . . [94 bracketed lines of the main text—and 134 lines in footnotes!] . . . "*D'opaque frondaison, de rayons et de fruits*" ("With thick foliage, with glinting lights and fruits"), which closes the canto. It might help to visualize each canto as somewhat like an onion: its pre-bracket opening lines, and post-bracket last lines (or in this case, last line), are its outer skin, the material between brackets one and two and between its penultimate and its final bracket, the next layer, between brackets two and three and the ante-penultimate and penultimate bracket, the next layer, and so on. As a way of distinguishing the different layers from each other, Roussel at one time considered having them printed in different colored inks, but he eventually abandoned this project because of the logistical difficulties and cost it would have entailed.[1]

I hope that what Roussel meant when he talked of the immense amount of time demanded by "*composition de vers de ce genre*" is becoming clear. The main text of each canto contains only one full stop, that which comes after the final line, although he does make frequent use of exclamation marks, question marks, and ellipses [. . .] as means of avoiding infringing this taboo. The only full stop allowed in a footnote, similarly, comes at its conclusion. Each single, vast, labyrinthine sentence hangs, therefore, from a single main verb: in Canto I, it comes in line 7 ("*Elles présentes, tout semble dater d'hier*" ["In their presence, everything seems to date from yesterday"]); in Canto II we have to wait

1. In 2004 Editions Al Dante published a sumptuous edition "*mise en couleurs*" by Jacques Sivan, with the text printed in black, green, white, purple, red, and yellow, on a grey background, and with the pages uncut along the top, as in the original Lemerre edition.

until the canto's penultimate line ("*Fait que . . .*" ["Makes . . ."]); in Canto III it is elided but implied in line 4 ("*Mais vers quoi ne courir . . .*" ["But what will a person not pursue . . ."]); and in Canto IV it occurs in line 1: "*je vois*"—which is the only time Roussel appears in person in the poem.

Like the vast majority of Roussel's poetry, *Nouvelles Impressions d'Afrique* is written in rhyming alexandrine couplets (i.e., twelve-syllable lines) that alternate masculine and feminine rhymes (in French, feminine rhymes end in a mute *e*, masculine rhymes don't). From the outset of his career as a poet Roussel established the habit of kick-starting composition by setting out a list of rhyming words down the right-hand side of the page, and in the very early "Mon Ame," published in 1897, a poem that unequivocally and unabashedly celebrates his own extraordinary literary talents, he figures his creative soul as a factory in which a vast army of workers extract from the fiery gulf of his inner being numerous "*rimes jaillissant en masse*" ("rhymes flying like masses of sparks"). By the time Roussel temporarily abandoned verse in his late 20s, to write the novels *Impressions d'Afrique* and *Locus Solus*, he had already composed around 25,000 lines in rhyming alexandrines; it seems to me likely that the ingenious constraints he imposed on himself when he took up verse again in 1915 were a practical way of disciplining his almost unstoppable poetic fluency.[2]

2. *La Doublure* (1897) is 5,586 lines long, and consists mainly of descriptions of the floats and large papier-mâché figures that feature in the annual carnival at Nice. (It was while composing *La Doublure* that Roussel experienced *la gloire* – see note to Canto III, line 94.) *La Vue* (1904) is made up of three poems, "La Vue" (which runs to over 2,000 lines), "Le Concert," and "La Source (both just over 1,000 lines each), in which Roussel describes in impossible detail the tiny scenes reproduced in the lens of a pen-holder ("La Vue"), in the sketch of a hotel adorning a sheet of hotel writing paper ("Le Concert"), and on the label of a bottle of mineral water ("La Source"). In 1989 a trunk containing nine cartons full of Roussel's papers was discovered in a warehouse of the Société Bedel, a furniture storage company, and among many surprises were two enormously long poems, *La Seine* and *Les Noces*, which date from the first ten years of Roussel's writing career. *La Seine* (probably 1900-1903) is 6,931 lines long, and the unfinished *Les Noces* (probably 1904-8) is 8,760 lines long, although two further sections remained to be written. Both have been published in Pauvert/Fayard's ongoing edition of Roussel's

If, from one angle, the brackets and footnotes of *Nouvelles Impressions d'Afrique* insistently disrupt and disjoin, frustrating, with their seemingly endless digressions and lists of examples, the reader's urge for completion, from another they serve as forms of connection, like railway points, that enable the poem to cross over into whole new regions of proliferating analogy and illustration. Sometimes these switchovers occur in rapid succession. In Canto III, for instance, Roussel offers a list of the different ways in which various people make lots of money in America; one person does so by selling heaps of pictures to a snobbish stockbroker:

Soit que par stocks on vende à l'agioteur snob
(((Le rôle du snobisme ((((au vrai qu'était Jacob?[1]

1. Même est-on sûr que Dieu, quand il fit le snobisme
   (Si l'animal ne sait pas plus percer un isthme . . .

Whether one sells in heaps to the speculator who's a snob
(((The role played by snobbery ((((in essence, what was Jacob?[1]

1. Can one even be sure that God, when he made snobbery
   (If animals no more know how to build a canal across an isthmus . . .

(lines 55–56 and footnote 1, lines 1–2)

This is the poem's most accelerated series of transitions: the triple bracket introduces the assertion that snobbery will always play a major role in life, and the quadruple bracket the novel idea that Jacob—and Esau too!—were snobs in their wrangling over a birthright; the footnote launches the notion that God possibly made animals snobs as well as men, and the first bracket within the footnote ponders the relationship between men and animals, who may not be able to build a canal across an isthmus or do various other things that men can do—

complete works, *La Seine* (as volume III, edited by Patrick Besnier) in 1994 and *Les Noces* (as volumes V and VI, edited by Pierre Bazantay) in 1998.

but aren't we a bit like pigs, this particular parenthesis closes, or life-saving dogs?

> *Ne retrouvons-nous pas nos instincts chez les porcs?*
> *Chez les chiens sauveteurs qui foncent à la nage?),*

> Do we not rediscover our own instincts in pigs?
> In life-saving dogs when they plunge into the water?),
> (Footnote 1, lines 8–9)

Like much of Roussel's best writing, *Nouvelles Impressions d'Afrique* is extremely funny, and beautiful, but its humor and beauty are not easy to define. Reading through the vast collection of his manuscripts housed in the Fonds Roussel in the Manuscript Department of the old Bibliothèque Nationale on Rue Richelieu in order to write my critical biography of him (*Raymond Roussel and the Republic of Dreams* [2001]), I occasionally wondered if he suffered from Asperger's syndrome, or a mild form of autism. He had, to quote Robert Desnos, "*[un] esprit amoureux de logique,*" a phrase Desnos used when recalling a meeting between Roussel and his publisher Désiré Lemerre during the First World War, which Roussel spent as a soldier of the *deuxième classe* in the 13th Vincennes Artillery regiment. When Lemerre came across Roussel he was counting petrol cans; Desnos writes:

> The cataclysm stupefied him. His highly logical mind could not conceive of such an enterprise. When asked what had most struck him in the course of those tragic years, he answered—and it was a profound thing to say—"I have never seen so many men."

This snapshot of the inordinately wealthy and supremely fastidious dandy caught up in the theatre of war is particularly interesting in the context of the genesis of *Nouvelles Impressions d'Afrique*, which, despite the somewhat misleading account Roussel gives of the poem's origins in "Comment j'ai écrit certains de mes livres," was indubitably being composed in the form that we know it by mid-1916 at the latest.[3] I wouldn't want to suggest that *Nouvelles Impressions d'Afrique* is a war poem, though a machine gun briefly appears in a footnote in Canto III, and a blindfolded army emissary features twice (Canto II, line 327, Canto III, lines 18–19) and in a Zo illustration [no. 27]). To what extent Roussel's experiences at the front were a catalyst for the way *Nouvelles Impressions* uses "parentheses as a means of making language disintegrate," as Michel Leiris puts it, is impossible to know, but the poem's frankness about its own conceptual framework (whereas Roussel kept the *procédé* underpinning his fiction and plays a strict secret),[4] and its many scatological images, do suggest the

3. In "Comment j'ai écrit certains de mes livres" Roussel suggests that *Nouvelles Impressions d'Afrique* started out life as a poem in the mode of the three poems collected in *La Vue*:

> It concerned a tiny pair of opera-glasses to be worn as a pendant, each of whose lenses, two millimeters in diameter and meant to be held very close to the eye, contained a photograph on glass—one of the bazaars of Cairo, the other of a quay in Luxor.
>
> I made a description in verse of these two photographs. (It was, in short, an exact sequel to my poem, *La Vue*.)
>
> Having completed this initial work, I took up the poem again from the beginning to polish the verses. But at the end of a certain time I realized that an entire lifetime would not be sufficient for this polishing, and I abandoned my task. This had in all taken me five years of work. If the manuscript could be retrieved from among my papers, it might perhaps prove interesting, such as it is, at least to certain of my readers.

Aside from a very brief fragment dating from 1906 set in an Egyptian bazaar, nothing of this sort has been recovered. On the other hand, throughout the First World War Roussel consistently dispatched drafts of work in progress to his business manager Eugène Leiris (the father of Michel Leiris) for safekeeping. Two of the envelopes that survive, those dated November 12, 1916, and March 2, 1917, contained manuscript drafts of *Nouvelles Impressions d'Afrique*, drafts that did not concern two photographs contained in miniature opera-glasses, but proved to be passages from Canto I and Canto II. On March 6, 1917 Roussel sent Leiris a typed draft of Canto I, which is reproduced in facsimile in the miscellaneous collection of Roussel's writings, *Épaves* (1972). This is simply a not yet fully expanded version of the canto as eventually published. This and the other early drafts reveal that the methodology of the poem was established from the outset, rather than in 1920, as Roussel's essay seems to suggest.

4. For an account of the *procédé*, see note to line 1 of footnote beginning at line 62 of Canto IV.

eruption of certain energies that had previously been repressed. "What sluice gates," as the devoted Roussel critic Jean Ferry has pointedly asked, "broke in him, allowing these malodorous jets to burst forth?"[5]

The quick-fire transitions of the lines quoted from Canto III are not, however, typical of the experience the poem as a whole offers. Roussel seems to have set himself an upper limit of five brackets, and although opening and closing pages present a flurry of opening and closing parentheses, there are long stretches in the middle of all of the cantos in which we forget about the poem's peculiar structure, and are allowed to enjoy in peace the pleasures of the list. The punctuation marks that serve his turn here, and which feature far more often than the bristling bracket, are the semicolon and the dash. Roussel is one of the great exponents of the list in poetry, a rival of earlier great list-makers such as Christopher Smart or Walt Whitman. If the parenthesis is a means of interrupting or re-angling a train of thought, with the promise, always fulfilled, of returning to it, the list is Roussel's way of expanding the digression the parenthesis introduces, on some occasions until it seems the list will stretch on, like the kings born of Banquo's seed paraded by the witches before the eyes of the appalled Macbeth, "to th' crack of doom." These lists are often launched by an appeal to analogy as occurs, for instance, at line 20 of Canto I. Roussel has been describing how a person having his photograph taken stays as still as possible, but nevertheless wonders, should he move even a little bit, if his image will come out blurred:

—*Se demandant, pour peu qu'en respirant il bouge,*
Si sur la gélatine, à la lumière rouge,
Dans le révélateur il apparaîtra flou,—

5. Jean Ferry published two indispensable guides to *Nouvelles Impressions d'Afrique*: *Une étude sur Raymond Roussel* (Paris: Arcanes, 1953), which presents a line-by-line commentary on Canto III, and *Une autre étude sur Raymond Roussel* (Paris: Publications du Collège de Pataphysique, 1964), which offers a somewhat less detailed analysis of the other cantos. I, and all other Roussel scholars, are much indebted to Ferry's pioneering researches.

((((Tels se demandent:—S'il diffère d'un filou,
Le fat qui d'un regard . . .

—Wondering, even if he moves only by breathing,
Whether on the gelatin photographic plate, in the red light,
In the developing fluid he will appear blurred,—
((((Such also wonder:—If he differs from a thief,
The fop who with one glance . . .

There follow after the example of this penniless fop, who, having just married a rich prostitute, wonders if he's any better than a thief, 53 further instances of people, animals, and things (including a lamppost, a thermometer, a billiard ball, the sole of a shoe, hot milk, and a wall) presented in analogous states of wondering. The list runs, with two further embedded brackets, and two footnotes as well, to line 135, and an astronomer wondering if he'll ever see a man walking upside down on the moon like a fly on the ceiling.

But this list is as nothing to that offered in Canto II, the Everest, or perhaps that should be the Great Pyramid, of *Nouvelles Impressions d'Afrique*. At 642 lines, Canto II is ten lines longer than the other three cantos put together, and 416 of these lines are occupied by a list that offers 207 examples of small things that might be mistaken for bigger things with which they have a visual similarity. For instance, to quote the first:

—l'appareil qui, trouvé par Franklin,
Sans danger dans un puits fait se perdre la foudre
Pour un fil gris passé dans une aiguille à coudre;

—the apparatus that, discovered by Franklin,
Makes lightning disappear harmlessly into a pit,
For a grey thread passed through the eye of a needle;

(lines 91–93)

Many of the examples in this list are presented in extremely condensed language, and Roussel's French can take some time to puzzle out:

> —*pour le goinfre à refrain*
> *Qu'à force d'applaudir on prend, le cousin braque*
> *Qui fonce en plein plafond;*
>
> (lines 215–17)

The "*goinfre à refrain*," the one who keeps guzzling, is a mosquito, and he is taken, or really killed, by a clap of the hands, "*à force d'applaudir*"; this mosquito is visually similar to, but smaller than, "*le cousin braque*," the crazy daddy longlegs who speeds about up by the ceiling.

Roussel's examples and images, I think it's worth pointing out here, all work. There is no more room for ambiguity or readerly "interpretation" in this poem than in a crossword puzzle; there is a correct solution to each vignette. *Nouvelles Impressions d'Afrique* is, among other things, as Michel Leiris pointed out, a vast *casse-tête*, or brain-teaser, and one of the central principles underlying my version of it can be illustrated by the way I have rendered the lines above:

> —for the persistently guzzling mosquito
> Whom one kills with a clap of the hands, the crazy daddy longlegs
> Who speeds about up by the ceiling;

My dominant intention was to offer the reader a precise and accurate "crib"; my translation is designed to make Roussel's French comprehensible, and I have not, on occasion, scrupled to expand what in the original is compressed to the point of obscurity. Where necessary, I have offered supplementary expositions of particularly knotted images in the notes, which also explain the various allusions the poem makes to such as Aesop, La Fontaine, and Pierre Corneille. All translators of poetry face hard choices. There is no way a version of *Nouvelles Impressions* can both be accurate and recreate the poem's rhythm or rhyme scheme, without straying very far indeed from idiomatic English; my determination to make Roussel's meaning as clear as possible has resulted in some sacrifice of his extraordinary concision, though this can always be savoured by glancing across at the French on the facing page.[6] My version does, however, allow the Anglophone reader full access to the dizzying inventiveness, the uncanny feats of connection and visual analogy, with which he fulfilled the poem's mind-boggling overarching conceit.

Roussel's imagination, as *Nouvelles Impressions d'Afrique* so dramatically demonstrates, was both severely logical and disconcertingly unboundaried. His "*œil curieux*," to use a phrase from the early long poem "La Vue," discerns, in this long central list in Canto II, similarities that are both compellingly exact and deliriously far-fetched:

> —*pour un œuf au plat seul à l'écart,*
> *Salé ferme à son centre, un baissé crâne à rite*
> *D'âgé prêtre à jaunisse;*

> —for a single fried egg, on its own,
> With a vigorously salted yolk, the skull, bent in prayer,
> Of an old priest with jaundice;

(lines 111-13)

> —*Pour ce qu'un tousseur montre au docteur pour la gorge,*
> *Un cavernaire arceau, par le couchant rougi,*
> *A stalactite unique;*

> —For that which someone with a cough shows to a throat doctor,
> [ie. an inflamed uvula]
> An arched cavern, reddened by the setting sun,
> With a solitary stalactite;

(lines 289–91)

---

6. Two earlier translators of Roussel have attempted to match the constraints of the original: see Kenneth Koch's version in rhyming hexameter couplets of Canto III (first published in 1964, and reprinted in *How I Wrote Certain of My Books* (ed. Trevor Winkfield, Exact Change, 1995), and Ian Monk's version of the entire poem in pentameter couplets (Atlas Press, 2004).

The serene lack of affect with which Roussel presents such comparisons is a characteristic of the poem as a whole; and it is this rigorous impersonality which enables the poem to range so freely from the minute—a crumb caught between two teeth—to the cosmic, the "*profondeurs du grand vide céleste*" to which the astronomer at the end of Canto IV grows accustomed, and which Roussel selected as the subject for the last of Zo's illustrations (no. 59): "A section of starry sky without any earthly landscape as if seen from some vantage point in space and giving the impression of infinity."

The illustrations for *Nouvelles Impressions d'Afrique* were not the first commission Henri-A. Zo had received from Roussel. During the premier of *L'Étoile au front* at the Vaudeville Theatre on May 5, 1924, a pitched battle broke out between Roussel's vociferous surrealist admirers, who that day included André Breton, Roger Vitrac, Michel Leiris, and Robert Desnos, and the more conservative, but equally vociferous, sections of the audience who were outraged by the play's oddness. As Roussel recalls in "Comment j'ai écrit certains de mes livres":

> Another tumult, another battle, but this time my supporters were far more numerous. During the third act the furor reached such a pitch that the curtain had to be lowered, and was only raised again after a considerable interval.
>
> During the second act, one of my opponents cried out to those who were applauding, "Go it, you hired band of clappers" ["*Hardi la claque*"], to which Robert Desnos replied: "We are the hired band of clappers/the slap, and you are the cheek" ["*Nous sommes la claque et vous êtes la joue*"]. This witticism caught on, and was quoted in various papers.

Roussel was so pleased with Desnos's punning riposte that he commissioned Zo (who had illustrated a novel by one of Roussel's great literary heroes, Pierre Loti) to paint a diptych featuring, on one side, the battle raging in the auditorium during the first night of Victor Hugo's *Hernani*, and on the other the similar scenes that disrupted the premier of *L'Étoile au front*. A bronze plaque inscribed with Desnos's jest was affixed to the bottom of the frame.

But on this second occasion Zo had no contact with the author himself; he received his instructions[7] for the fifty-nine illustrations that were to embellish *Nouvelles Impressions d'Afrique*, and establish his own claim on the attentions of posterity, not from Roussel, but through the intermediary of a detective agency called Agence Goron. He was informed, further, that he would not be allowed to read the poem for which his fifty-nine Chinese ink drawings were commissioned until after its publication. When Zo eventually found out the name of his employer, he at once fired off a letter of remonstrance:

> Please allow me to tell you that I bitterly regret the fact you wanted this collaboration to be shrouded in such an impenetrable mystery. These are not the pictures I would have made if I had known I was illustrating Raymond Roussel!

In this letter he also complains that the precision of the instructions he received meant his drawings "*manquent de liberté, de fantasie,*" and he goes on to wish that Roussel had agreed to engage with him in a genuine collaboration:

> my illustrations . . . would have been more in harmony with your work if I'd been able to read the text, or had the honor of knowing the personality of the poet.

Clearly it was the prospect of just this sort of interaction that Roussel went to such lengths to avoid.

For Salvador Dalí, who considered *Nouvelles Impressions d'Afrique*

---

7. Roussel's "*indications*" or instructions to Zo were preserved by the foreman at Lemerre's printing house, Eugène Vallée. After Roussel's death Vallée passed these on to Michel Leiris, who published them in the magazine *Cahiers G.L.M.* in March of 1939. The instructions are not to be considered as captions, for they were not included in the original Lemerre edition. For a comprehensive discussion of each picture and its relation to Roussel's text, see Laurent Busine's *Raymond Roussel: Contemplator enim* (La Lettre volé, 1995).

the most "ungraspably poetic" book of the era, the choice of illustrations was further testimony "to the genius of Raymond Roussel." Their "militant banality," to use a phrase of John Ashbery's, contrasts powerfully with the strangeness of the poem confronting the reader, yet also matches its immersion in a generalized commonality. The pictures themselves are as mundane as illustrations in an early twentieth-century encyclopedia (and the portrait of Amerigo Vespucci is closely based, as Roussel's instruction suggested it might be, on the picture of the explorer in the *Nouveau Larousse illustré*), but in the context of the poem from which the images are drawn, the characters and scenes that Zo presents come to seem, in their very ordinariness, hauntingly singular too. Among Roussel initiates there has been much speculation, which was started by Michel Leiris in an essay published in 1939 entitled "Autour des *Nouvelles Impressions d'Afrique*," about Roussel's choice of images for illustration, and all lovers of the poem will have their favorite. My own is no. 52:

> A walker, with his arm raised and his fingers open, who has just dropped a pebble (which is still visible) down a well, inclining his head as if to listen out for the splash (no other people).

By some strange coincidence, the rambler Zo drew in response to this instruction bears a ghostly resemblance to the Roussel of a series of photographs he had taken attired in one of his most elegant outfits at Carlsbad in 1912.

Undoubtedly one reason Roussel decided to have each page of his poem twinned with an illustration was to increase the bulk of the volume. The 160 worksheets relating to the composition of *Nouvelles Impressions d'Afrique* preserved in the Bibliothèque Nationale truly reveal the immense amount of time demanded by verse of this kind, and some sheets record at the foot of the page his punishing work schedule: "11 h sam. 8 dim. 9¼ lundi. 10¼ mardi. 12¼ merc . . ." Still, at the end of these long years of dedicated industry, his poem remained dispiritingly short. Proofs were first printed off in 1927, and like Proust, Roussel used these to expand and revise.[8] Clearly he wanted the book, the last whose production he would be able to oversee, to resemble in size its predecessor (in name at least), *Impressions d'Afrique*, and yet in its final form the text ran to only fifty-nine pages. Zo's illustrations double that, and Roussel's decision to leave all the versos blank doubles that again. Further, he thought fit to reprint after *Nouvelles Impressions d'Afrique*, his last published poem, his first "Mon Ame" (not included here), in which he announced the arrival of his fecund genius to the world, or at least to readers of the July 12, 1897 edition of *Le Gaulois*.[9] Its title, however, became "L'Ame de Victor Hugo," and he now introduced it with the following explanation: "One night I dreamed I saw Victor Hugo writing at his desk, and this is what I read as I leaned over his shoulder." It must have been with extreme reluctance that Roussel projected onto Victor Hugo, with whom Zo's diptych had already surreptitiously aligned him, the glorious reception that he had anticipated for himself. Traces, however, remain of the poem's original subject: Roussel couldn't bring himself to change a reference to his idolatrous admirers, his *roussellâtres*, to *hugoâtres*, leaving instead a blank followed by *lâtres* ("*Sans souci de ces   lâtres / Qui me mettent au rang des dieux*"); and the poem's penultimate verse similarly gestures back to the original predictions Roussel had made in it, and which he now had to acknowledge had been spectacularly misguided:

A cette explosion voisine
De mon génie universel
Je vois le monde qui s'incline
Devant ce nom: Victor Hugo.

8. Roussel had so many sets of proofs drawn up for him that in June of 1931 Eugène Vallée had to write to him asking him to destroy all earlier sets of proofs to prevent confusion. Roussel failed to comply with this request. He was, however, popular with employees of the firm involved in the production of his books, for he used to offer cash rewards to anyone who spotted a misprint.

9. The poem was prefaced by a headnote, almost certainly written by Roussel himself, informing the reader that the poem was composed three years earlier when the author was just seventeen, and adding, "one can judge from that fact the sort of promise his precocious and fecund genius holds for the future."

> At the explosion deriving
> From my universal genius
> I see the world bow
> Before this name: Victor Hugo.

Does Victor Hugo rhyme with *universel*? No, but it's not hard to think of a name that does.

The phrase *"Pas de personnages"* recurs repeatedly in Roussel's instructions to Zo. Like the inventor Martial Canterel, the hero of *Locus Solus* (1914), Roussel lived an essentially solitary life, ensconced behind the walls of his extensive property in Neuilly, embarking alone on travels in the footsteps of Pierre Loti, or having himself chauffeured around Europe in his custom-built *roulotte*, a kind of luxurious caravan of which he was so proud that when he visited Rome he set about arranging for both the Pope and Mussolini to inspect it.[10] *Nouvelles Impressions d'Afrique* was the last of the literary experiments with which Roussel hoped to dazzle and delight a mass audience, and like all his earlier books, despite the usual well-funded barrage of publicity, it failed to render him the toast of Paris. These poems, as Robert Desnos cautiously advised him, *"sont faits pour l'éternité plus que pour la popularité."* The demands they make on the reader are considerable, but I can confidently assert that they offer a challenge and an experience unique in literature. Although only 59 pages long, they seem to compress an entire lifetime's involvement in the bizarre and banal ways of the world, and a vast selection of the things, natural and artificial, that make it up, and the different media through which they impinge on us, into an all-accommodating, yet rigorously conceived and executed poetic symphony. The form of each canto means its end inevitably returns us to its opening, and this return creates a moment fraught with the sweet mel-

---

10. In December of 1926 Roussel wrote from Rome to his paid companion Charlotte Dufrène: "Mussolini came and spent a long time visiting the *roulotte*; he is very simple and very kind. I also had a long audience with the Pope, to whom I showed some photos of the *roulotte*, and who kept them (Mussolini, also, so now I have none left)." Roussel had hoped the Pope would inspect his vehicle in person, but had to be content with exhibiting it to the Papal Nuncio, who departed *"émerveillé."*

ancholy pang of simultaneous completion and loss. Images of extinction and decay increasingly invade Canto IV, which is dominated by a long list of fires that go out, a list that can't help but summon up the death in Sicily awaiting Roussel less than a year after the poem finally saw the light of day:

> *chez l'homme,*
> *Le feu de l'œil s'éteint à l'âge où dent par dent*
> *Et cheveu par cheveu, sans choc, sans accident,*
> *Par l'action du temps, sa tête se déleste;*

> with men
> The fire in the eye goes out at the age when tooth by tooth
> And hair by hair, without shock or accident,
> By the mere action of time, the head is slowly unburdened;
>
> (lines 88–91)

Roussel never lived to see the literary glory he predicted for himself in "Mon Ame," and despite acquiring over the years numerous eminent admirers, including such as André Breton, Marcel Duchamp, Salvador Dalí, Alain Robbe-Grillet, Raymond Queneau, Michel Foucault, Georges Perec, and John Ashbery, his work remains something of a cult secret. Readers of this edition of *Nouvelles Impressions d'Afrique* will, I hope, be persuaded that Roussel was indeed one of the "*élu*" irradiated by "*le saint feu du génie,*" a writer entitled to find

> *au firmament les vrais astres piteux*
> *Auprès de l'astre neuf qui sur son front rayonne*

> the real stars in the sky pitiful
> In comparison with the new star that shines on his forehead
>
> (Canto IV, lines 72–73).

Mark Ford

Abbreviations

The following abbreviations are used in the Notes:

CJ *Comment j'ai écrit certains de mes livres* by Raymond Roussel (Pauvert, 1963; L'imaginaire Gallimard, no. 324, 1995)

RC *Roussel & Co.* by Michel Leiris (Fata Morgana/Fayard, 1998)

RD *Raymond Roussel and the Republic of Dreams* by Mark Ford (Faber, 2000; Cornell University Press, 2001)

RR *Raymond Roussel* by François Caradec (Fayard, 1997)

UE *Une étude sur Raymond Roussel* by Jean Ferry (Arcanes, 1953)

I

Damiette

LA MAISON OU SAINT LOUIS FUT PRISONNIER

Sans doute à réfléchir, à compter cela porte,
D'être avisé que là, derrière cette porte,
Fut trois mois prisonnier le roi saint! . . . Louis neuf! . . .
Combien le fait, pourtant, paraît tangible et neuf
En ce pays jonché de croulantes merveilles,   5
Telles qu'on n'en sait point ici-bas de plus vieilles!

I

Damietta

THE HOUSE WHERE SAINT LOUIS WAS HELD PRISONER

Without doubt to ponder, to register this truth is momentous,
To be informed that there, behind that door,
The saintly king was for three months a prisoner! . . . Louis IX! . . .
How this fact, however, seems tangible and new
In this country strewn with crumbling marvels
So old that no one knows of any on earth that are older!

Damiette: Port on the Mediterranean coast of Egypt.

Saint Louis: Louis IX (1215–1270) embarked on his crusade (the Seventh Crusade) to the Holy Land in 1248. He was captured after being defeated at the Battle of Mansoura in 1250, and held captive in the house of Ibrahim ben Lokman, the secretary of the Sultan, until a ransom of 400,000 *livres* was paid.

5   *En ce pays*: Roussel first visited Egypt in 1906, when he was 29. Accompanied by his personal physician, Doctor Mattin, he took a three-and-a-half-week boat trip down the Nile. A journal he kept of this trip survives, but reveals little about his personal responses to the *"croulantes merveilles"* scattered about the land; this is how he relates their excursion to the Valley of the Kings on December 2: "Crossed the Nile by boat—Hired donkeys—Went to see the Valley of the Kings—Cold lunch—sun—heat." He mentions none of the locations featured in *Nouvelles Impressions d'Afrique*. This journal is reproduced in full in *Digraphe* (no. 67, Feb. 1994, pp. 125–36). (For a detailed consideration of the role played by Egypt in Roussel's imaginative development, see *RD*, pp. 90–102.)

Saint Louis in his prison
in Damietta. (line 3)

Elles présentes, tout semble dater d'hier:
Le nom dont, écrasé, le porteur est si fier
Que de mémoire, à fond, il sait sans une faute
(Comme sait l'occupant, dans une maison haute,   10
D'un clair logis donnant sur le dernier palier
—Photographe quelconque habile à pallier
Pattes d'oie et boutons par de fins stratagèmes—
((Pouvoir du retoucheur! lorsque arborant ses gemmes
(((Chacun, quand de son moi, dont il est entiché,   15
Rigide, il fait tirer un orgueilleux cliché,
—Se demandant, pour peu qu'en respirant il bouge,
Si sur la gélatine, à la lumière rouge,
Dans le révélateur il apparaîtra flou,—
((((Tels se demandent:—S'il diffère d'un filou,   20
Le fat qui d'un regard (((((parfois une étincelle,
L'entourant de pompiers qui grimpent à l'échelle,
Fait d'un paisible immeuble un cratère qui bout[1];)))))

---

1. Que n'a-t-on, lorsqu'il faut d'un feu venir à bout,
   Un géant bon coureur,—quand une maison flambe,
   Un sauveteur loyal doit-il, traînant la jambe,
   Considérer de loin la besogne en boudeur?—

In their presence, everything seems to date from yesterday:
The name of which the owner, now crushed, is so proud
That he knows absolutely and by heart, without a single fault
(As well as he who occupies a bright apartment,
In a tall building, which opens onto the top landing, knows
—Some photographer who is skillful at palliating
Crow's feet and spots by clever stratagems—
((Power of the retoucher! when, sporting her jewels,
(((Each person, infatuated with self-love, when he proudly has
Someone take his photograph, keeping as still as he can,
—Wondering, even if he moves only by breathing,
Whether on the gelatin photographic plate, in the red light,
In the developing fluid he will appear blurred,—
((((Such also wonder:—If he differs from a thief,
The fop who with one glance (((((sometimes a spark,
Causing firemen, climbing ladders, to surround it,
Makes of a peaceful block of flats a boiling crater[1])))))),

1. How one needs, when it comes to putting out a fire,
   A giant who is a good runner,—when a house is ablaze,
   Should a loyal rescuer, dragging his limbs,
   Sulkily consider his task from afar?—

9   *sans une faute*: Some 216 lines (including those in the footnotes) elapse before we learn what the proud bearer of an ancient name knows so faultlessly: to complete the opening syntactic unit of Canto I, turn to the last four lines, 169–72.

13   *fins stratagèmes*: To learn what the photographer who lives on the top floor of his building knows so well, turn to line 168.

14   *lorsque arborant ses gemmes*: Roussel completes this second parenthesis in lines 165–67.

19   *il apparaîtra flou*: This train of thought is returned to at line 136. There we are informed that the person having his photograph taken, and wondering if his image will be blurred if he moves, "*Prétend déterminer son rang ou ses talents*" ("Assertively presents his rank or his talents") by dressing up in an appropriate costume.

20   *((((Tels se demandent*: The first of the "hooks" which Roussel uses in *Nouvelles Impressions d'Afrique* to present a series of examples illustrating or analogous to a particular act or state. The person having his photograph taken "wonders," if he moves, if he'll come out blurred, and this serves to introduce 54 instances of people and things in comparable states of wondering: the fop who has just married a rich prostitute, if he's better than a thief, the new arrival at Nice if he should dress in linen, through to the astronomer of lines 133–35, who wonders if he'll see a man walking on the moon through his telescope.

23   *bout[1];))))*: The poem's footnotes are to be read immediately, since their rhymes connect with those of the main text ("*bout / bout*," "*opportune / fortune*").

> A house that is ablaze surrounded
> by firemen climbing ladders.
> (lines 21–23)

Enflamma, dépourvu, lui, de toute fortune,
Une catin de marque ayant voiture, hôtel,   25
Qu'il vient, le rouge au front, de conduire à l'autel;
—A Nice, l'arrivant, l'œil sur le thermomètre,
Si, défiant le rhume, en toile il va se mettre[1];
—Resté seul, Horace, à quelle vitesse fuir;
—Le lièvre si lorsqu'il musait par la bruyère   30
L'eût distancé même un vieux morceau de gruyère;
—Si valsent ou non les bouteilles de Clicquot
Le soupeur dont le nez tourne au coquelicot;

Qui, prêt, tel Gulliver, à vaincre sa pudeur,   5
Aurait à satisfaire une envie opportune.

1. A l'hiverneur niçois donner un pardessus
(Prêt qu'il est à jurer—les jours même où, pansus,
De durs magots de neige y pouffent d'un air nice—
Qu'en janvier, de bon cœur, on irait nu dans Nice,
Tel Archimède aux cent coups criant: « Eurêka »),   5
C'est donner:—au novice, en mer, de l'ipéca,
Tandis qu'à la briser l'ouragan tend l'écoute;
—Quand un conférencier prélude, à qui l'écoute,
Un narcotique;—à qui hors d'un train bon marcheur
Se penche, un éventail;—lorsqu'il rentre, au pêcheur   10

Himself destitute of all fortune, inflamed

A well-known prostitute, owner of a car and a large townhouse,

Whom he has just, blushing all over, led to the altar;

—The new arrival in Nice, his eye on the thermometer,

If, scorning the danger of catching a cold, he will wear linen[1];

—Horace, left alone, at what speed he will flee;

—The hare if, while he was dawdling in the heather,

Even an old piece of gruyère might have outpaced him;

—The diner whose nose is turning poppy-red

If the bottles of Clicquot are waltzing or not;

Who, provided he's ready, like Gulliver, to overcome his modesty,

Would be able to satisfy an opportune bodily urge.

1. To give an overcoat to someone who winters at Nice

(Prepared as he is to swear—even on days when pot-bellied

Hard-packed snowmen grin in a friendly manner there—

That in Nice one could easily go about naked in January,

Like Archimedes excitedly crying "Eureka!"),

Is like giving:—an emetic to the novice at sea,

Just as the hurricane stretches the sail to breaking point;

—When a lecturer begins, to whoever's listening,

A narcotic;—to someone who is leaning out of a fast train,

A fan;—to the sinner, when he returns

Footnote 1 (from previous page), line 5 *tel Gulliver*: In Book 1, chapter 5 of Jonathan Swift's *Gulliver's Travels* (1726), Gulliver douses a fire raging in the Lilliputian royal apartments by urinating on the flames.

27   *A Nice*: Roussel attended the carnival in Nice each winter throughout his teens. His first book, *La Doublure,* written when he was eighteen and published in 1897, is a novel in verse whose 5,586 lines consist almost entirely of descriptions of the floats and *têtes de carton* that feature in the carnival's parade. He returned to the topic in various later poems, including "L'Inconsolable" and "Têtes de Carton du Carnaval de Nice" (both published in 1904 and collected in *Comment j'ai écrit certains de mes livres* [1935]).

Footnote 1, line 6 *C'est donner*: The 23 instances that follow illustrate the folly of giving something to someone who doesn't want or need it. It's pointless to give someone wintering in Nice an overcoat because he will always claim it's warm enough not to need one, even if it has snowed and the city is full of snowmen, like that illustrated by Zo. It's equally pointless, the note goes on to explain, to give an emetic to a novice at sea in a storm, because he'll already be vomiting; a narcotic to someone in the audience when a lecturer is about to start, since he'll already be almost asleep; or an aphrodisiac to someone being hanged, since he'll already have an erection.

29   *Resté seul, Horace*: Pierre Corneille's play *Horace* (1640) is set in ancient Rome. The hero and his two brothers must fight the three Curiace brothers from Alba, with which Rome is at war. After his two brothers are killed Horace treacherously flees, then kills the Curiace brothers one by one.

30   *Le lièvre*: An allusion to Aesop's fable "The Hare and the Tortoise," adapted by La Fontaine in his *Fables choisies* of 1688.

A snowman, such as children
make, with its mouth wide open,
seemingly bursting out laughing.
(footnote 1, lines 2–3)

—L'Yankee si, pour de bon, plus lisse est qu'une orange

Ayant communié tard, de la noix vomique;
—Un nez postiche au juif, moins que le sien comique;
—Pendant l'ivresse, avant le serrement complet,
Un aphrodisiaque au pendu;—le soufflet
A qui s'escrime contre un feu de cheminée   15
Réfractaire;—à qui sort d'un livre, auguste aînée,
Une idyllique fleur sèche, un aplatissoir;
—A qui, sagace, en paix laisse une aragne un soir,
S'assurant une passe heureuse, un porte-chance;
—Lorsque en gants de peau vers l'eau bénite elle avance   20
Son médius rebelle, à la dévote, un truc
Pour ne rien gaspiller;—quand l'express, truck par truck,
Brûle en route un marchand train, à qui voit leur lutte,
Un pronostic;—le soir venu, quand, dans sa hutte,
Pour son somme il s'apprête, au noir, des bigoudis;   25
—Quand, martelant le sol, dans ses doigts engourdis
Souffle un mal inspiré dyspeptique, une boule
Puante à qui de près lui parle;—un jour sans houle,
De l'avance au vapeur qu'oseur brave un voilier;
—Au piéton qu'un sellé cheval sans cavalier   30
Dépasse, un coup double à demi-tour sur l'échine;
—A l'ouvrière, en juin, qui, cousant sans machine,
Se tette une phalange, une rose à tenir;

—If the world is really smoother than an orange,

From having at last taken communion, the laxative *nux vomica*;
—To the Jew a false nose less comic than his own;
—During his delirium, before his strangling is complete,
An aphrodisiac to the man being hanged;—bellows
To someone struggling with a fire that is out of control
In the hearth;—to he who takes from a book
An idyllic dried flower, august and venerable, a flatting hammer;
—To one who shrewdly leaves a spider in peace one evening,
Guaranteeing himself a spell of good fortune, a lucky charm;
—To the devout worshipper, a tip on how not to waste any,
When, wearing leather gloves, she advances towards the holy water
Her obstinate middle finger;—when the express train, car by car,
Tears past a goods train, to one who watches their race,
A forecast as to the outcome;—when in his hut at evening time
He's getting ready for sleep, to a black man, hair-curlers;
—When, stamping the ground, a dyspeptic has the bad idea
Of blowing into his frozen fingers, a stink ball
To whoever is speaking close to him;—on a windless day,
A headstart to the steamer that a sailboat boldly dares to a race;
—To the pedestrian whom a saddled but riderless horse
Overtakes, a double blow on the spine to make him about turn;
—To the seamstress who, in June, sewing without a machine,
Is sucking her finger, the stem of a rose to hold;

Footnote 1 (from previous page), line 11 *noix vomique*: The sinner who has just taken communion will want to keep the host in his body as long as possible. Roussel makes use of this idea again in Canto IV, line 81.

Footnote 1, lines 12 / 25 *Un nez postiche au juif / au noir, des bigoudis*: In his *Une autre étude sur Raymond Roussel*, Jean Ferry describes Roussel's anti-Semitism as "*épidermique*," or skin-deep. It reappears in the first footnote of Canto III (lines 29–30) which presents, as an example of things that are easy to recognize, a Jew with full lips, a hooked nose, and red-rimmed eyes, and in the figure of Booz Lévy of Act II, Scene 4 of *L'Étoile au front* (1925), who seduces the widow of the marquis d'Heucqueville by teaching a marmoset to use a clyster-pipe. Certainly the role played by Jews in his work is nugatory in comparison with that played by black Africans, such as the "*noir*" referred to at line 25 of this footnote, whose naturally curly hair means there's no point in giving him hair-curlers at night. For an illuminating discussion of Roussel's relation to turn-of-the-century French representations of Africa, see Annie Le Brun's *Vingt milles lieues sous les mots, Raymond Roussel* (1994), pp. 204–12.

A man taking a dried flower from a book. (footnote 1, lines 16–17)

La terre, alors qu'il grimpe à l'Alleghanys Range;   35
—L'étranger si plus rien n'est en *vice* amoral
Dans « vice-président » ou dans « vice-amiral »;
—Si, méthodique, avant de l'arroser, Cerbère
Le flairerait de ses trois nez, le réverbère;
—L'hiver, sur le trottoir, maudissant son bourreau,   40
S'il rentrera sans rhume, un riflard sans fourreau;
—Quand, poisseuse, elle a l'heur de puer, la semelle,
Si de son sort chanceux jalouse est sa jumelle;
—La fermière, à l'aube, en passant son caraco,
De quel coq debout la mit le cocorico;   45

—A rebours, lorsqu'il gronde avant d'intervenir,
Un coup de brosse au chien sur l'épine dorsale;   35
—Quand chez lui tout s'attaque, au maigre à langue sale
Qu'on va perdre, une forme à forcer les chapeaux;
—Au reclus, quand dehors claquent dur les drapeaux,
Sur la flûte, ondulant, maint chromatique exemple;
—Quand naît l'orage, à qui, dominé, le contemple   40
Et l'oit, pour moins que la lumière ailé le son;
—Au souffleur, quand tire à sa fin une chanson,
Lors du refrain un coup d'épaule à chaque ligne;
—Un sursis au coq qui, l'automne enfui, trépigne
Quand tarde une aube;—au Juif errant, un rond de cuir.   45

The Yankee climbing in the Allegheny Mountains;
—The foreigner if the term *vice* is completely amoral
In "vice-president" or "vice-admiral";
—If, before peeing on it, Cerberus would methodically
Sniff it with all three of his noses, the lamppost;
—In winter, on the pavement, cursing its torturer,
If it'll get home without a cold, the umbrella lacking its sheath;
—When a shoe sole is sticky, and has the good fortune to stink,
If its twin is jealous of its lucky fate;
—The farmer's wife, as she puts on her camisole in the dawn,
Which cock sang the cock-a-doodle-doo that woke her up;

—To a dog as he growls just before making
His move, a reverse brushstroke along his backbone;
—When all his organs fail, to the dirty-tongued and emaciated man
Who will soon die, a block for enlarging hats;
—To the recluse, when outside the flags are flapping hard,
Numerous flowing chromatic scales played on the flute;
—When the storm breaks, to whoever, captivated, watches it
And hears it, the information that sound travels less quickly than light;
—To the prompter, when a song nears its end,
A tap on the shoulder for each line of the refrain;
—A delay to a cock that, with the passing of autumn, prances with rage
At dawn's tardiness;—to the Wandering Jew, a round leather cushion.

A deserted street. In the foreground
a lamppost. (lines 38–39)

—Quand, sonore, entre en danse un conscrit, sa chemise,
Quelle purge, au réveil, dans la lampe il s'est mise;
—L'enfant qui de travers pousse dans le bassin,
S'il sera de sa mère, en naissant, l'assassin;
—La fleur, si son parfum renaîtra, qu'on asperge,   50
Sous un arbre écarté, d'un jet qui sent l'asperge;
—Lorsque à l'église un juif cherche un coin dans la nef,
Pourquoi chez Dieu bas on l'a mis, son couvre-chef;
—Le journal, qui le plus sur son revers pullule,
Du dentifrice, du prêt ou de la pilule;   55
—Réfléchissant sur son passé, si pour jeunot
Il passe, ou pour vieillot, le couteau de Janot;
—Le mur, quelle faute en conscience est la sienne,
Qu'exalté jouet du vent bat la persienne;
—L'archet, lorsque avant qu'il serve on retend son crin,   60
S'il faudra longtemps pour accorder le crincrin;
—Le thermomètre ailleurs placé que sous l'aisselle,
Si loin du but encore est la prochaine selle;
—S'il sera d'une douche honoré, le genou
Qu'en dada sédentaire a changé la nounou;   65
—Le procédé frappeur, pourquoi, fière, la bille
Point ne fraye avec lui, qui de rouge s'habille;
—Quel satisfait vient d'en sortir, celui qui sent

—When, with a fanfare, a conscript joins the dance, his shirt
What purgative he took at reveille by lamplight;
—The baby who is growing upside down in the womb,
If he'll be his mother's killer when he comes to be born;
—If its scent will ever recover, the flower being sprinkled,
Under an isolated tree, by a jet that smells of asparagus;
—A Jew, while he searches for a nook in a church nave,
Why, in the house of God, everyone takes off their hats;
—The newspaper, which teems more abundantly on its back page,
Ads for toothpaste, credit, or pills;
—Thinking about its past, if it passes for young
Or old, the knife of peasant Janot;
—What fault it has on its conscience, the wall
Which the shutter, passionate plaything of the wind, is beating;
—The bow, while before it is used its horsehair is re-stretched,
If it will take a long time for the fiddle to be tuned;
—The thermometer placed somewhere other than the armpit,
If the next stool is still a long way from its destination;
—If it will be honored with a drenching, the knee
That nurse has transformed into baby's rocking horse;
—The tip of the billiard cue as it strikes, why the proud ball
Which is red always refuses to have dealings with it;
—What satisfied man has just come out, the person who smells

46 *sonore*: i.e., with a fart.

57 *le couteau de Janot*: An allusion to a well-known fable about a French peasant who repeatedly replaces first the blade, then the handle of his knife.

62 *ailleurs placé que sous l'aisselle*: i.e., in the anus.

A wall that a slatted shutter bangs
in the wind (somewhere in the picture a
tossing tree giving the impression of a
storm). (lines 58–59)

Une odeur connue au seuil du numéro cent;
—Le collignon à fouet rageur, à quelle cote,   70
Dans le Grand Prix, gagnante, on donnerait Cocote;
—Si monter pratique en homme, à la longue, en arc,
Par degrés lui mettra les jambes, Jeanne d'Arc;
—Le sans le sou, s'il est près de rouler carrosse,
Qui, malin, d'un bossu vient de toucher la bosse;   75
—Quand sous sa dextre on penche un sac de confiseur,
Si des vers vont doubler son plaisir, le liseur;
—L'astronome âgé, si, gâteux, avec un signe
Du Zodiaque, un jour, il confondra le Cygne;
—Les vieux, si saint Martin, vraiment, par son été,   80
Rend possible un instant d'être et d'avoir été;
—L'architecte, si lorsqu'il porte, pas plus grosse
Qu'un jouet, sa maquette, on le prend pour un gosse;
—Le théologien, si la Vierge à son fils
Doit sa célébrité plus ou moins qu'à ses fils;   85
—Le dompteur, si sa veuve, un an, sans gris ni mauve,
Stricte s'habillera, dont se régale un fauve;
—Si ses enfants naîtront sourds, celle dont la main
Fut la veille accordée à son cousin germain;
—Le loustic, si, pour voir où son cordonnier perche,   90
Mieux vaut dans sa bottine ou son Bottin qu'on cherche;

A familiar scent on the threshold of a public toilet;
—The cabby with the ferocious whip, what odds
He might get on his gee-gee winning the Grand Prix;
—If mounting her horse like a man will, in the course of time,
Slowly make her bow-legged, Joan of Arc;
—The penniless man if he's about to start living in style,
After he's just wickedly touched the hump of a hunchback for luck;
—A bag of sweets dangling from his right hand, the prospective
Reader, if the packet's rhymes are going to double his pleasure;
—The ageing astronomer if, senile, he will one day mistake
A Swan electric light for a sign of the Zodiac;
—Old people if Saint Martin, on account of Saint Martin's summer, truly
Made possible an instant of being and of having been;
—The architect if, while he carries his model building that's no bigger
Than a toy, people will think he's a kid;
—The theologian if the Virgin owes her fame more to her son
Or to the gossamer known as *fils de la Vierge*;
—The animal tamer if his widow, one year on, without grey or mauve,
Will still be in strict mourning, as a wild beast eats him;
—If her children will be born deaf, she whose hand
The day before was given in marriage to her first cousin;
—The joker if, to find the address of his bootmaker,
It would be better to look inside his boot or in Bottin;

77   *des vers*: Roussel is referring to sweets that come wrapped in papers with rhyming mottos printed on them.

79   *le Cygne*: A reference to a light manufactured by the Swan Electric Light Company, founded in 1881.

91   *Bottin*: The name of a well-known street and trade directory.

Joan of Arc, seen from the front,
on horseback, in front of some foot
soldiers. (lines 72–73)

—Le lait chaud par l'attente attiédi dans son pot,
S'il choira dans la tasse avec ou sans sa peau;
—S'il risque, osé, qu'à grains d'ellébore on le purge
D'autorité, l'ultra-moderne dramaturge;
—Le poète, si l'on pourrait avec « Auteuil »
Faire à souhait rimer « comme dans un fauteuil »;
—Le peintre méconnu, si, du haut des étoiles,
Mort, il verra les snobs se disputer ses toiles;
—L'explorateur, si, loin de ce qu'il a de cher,
Un jour il repaîtra son prochain de sa chair;
—Si va lui sembler fort son enfant, l'accouchée
Qui ne s'est, avec lui, pas encore abouchée;
—Le jeune auteur[1],
Jusqu'à quand ses écrits paraîtront à ses frais[2];
—L'enfant, si, quand de l'ogre il mit les grosses bottes,
Poucet souffla dessus pour les rendre nabotes;
—Le vieillard qui parcourt une lettre de part,
S'il sera bientôt mûr, lui, pour le grand départ;

1.   La gloire a l'horreur du teint frais.
2.   Pour que d'un travailleur les œuvres soient illustres,
     Il faut que sur sa tête aient passé force lustres;
     Seul le chêne est prospère, envahissant, ombreux,
     Dont le tronc est strié de ronds déjà nombreux.

—Hot milk that has cooled while left in the pot,
If it will be poured into the cup with or without its skin;
—Should he daringly take a few grains of hellebore, if he'll be purged
Of his authority too, the ultra-modern dramatist;
—The poet if one can rhyme Auteuil
With armchair, as in "*comme dans un fauteuil*";
—The neglected painter if, from the stars,
Dead, he will see snobs arguing about his canvases;
—The explorer, far from all he holds dear, if
One day he will feed a fellow human being with his flesh;
—If her baby will seem strong, the mother who's just given birth
But not yet been reunited with her child;
—The young author[1]
For how long his writings will appear at his own expense[2];
—The child if, when he put on the ogre's huge boots,
Tom Thumb blew over them to make them tiny;
—The old man who glances at a letter announcing a death,
If he himself will soon be ready for the great departure;

---

1.   Glory has an aversion to fresh complexions.
2. For an industrious artist's work to be famous,
   He must be getting on in years;
   An oak tree is only flourishing, bushy, and shady
   If its trunk is already marked with many rings.

96   *Auteuil*: District in Paris.

105   *Jusqu'à quand ses écrits paraîtront à ses frais*: All Roussel's writings, from *La Doublure* of 1897 to the posthumous *Comment j'ai écrit certains de mes livres* (1935), were published at his own expense by the firm of Lemerre, founded in 1866 by Alphonse Lemerre. He paid enormous amounts to the company over the years, and Lemerre's exorbitant bills played a significant part in his eventual financial ruin.

107   *Poucet*: A reference to the fairy tale of Tom Thumb and the Seven League Boots, included in Charles Perrault's *Contes de ma mère l'Oye, ou histories du temps passé* (1697). When Tom Thumb puts on the giant's boots, they shrink to the size of his own feet.

A very old and very bushy oak tree.
(footnote 2, lines 3–4)

—Le Président, quels points il rend à la solive 110
Alors qu'il signe ou gâche en discours sa salive;
—L'ouvrier qui se sait un clou dans l'estomac,
S'il le retrouvera demain dans son thomas;
—Le convive en retard risquant l'excuse louche,
Si l'on va rapporter la soupière et la louche; 115
—A quel prix bout par bout sera par lui vendu
L'homicide licol, l'héritier d'un pendu;
—La poule, comment, l'œuf qu'elle venait de pondre,
Avec l'œuf d'une cane elle a pu le confondre;
—L'ignorant qui voit fuir vers le large un bateau[1] 120
Dont seul émerge encore un fragment de mâture,
Si des squales déjà son monde est la pâture;
—De qui sont ses marmots, la fille dont le lit,
Tant elle a de savoir, jamais ne désemplit;
—L'amateur de morphine, à quel rang Épicure, 125
En classant les plaisirs, eût placé la piqûre;
—L'alpiniste en extase au bord d'une hauteur,
Comment de l'univers louer assez l'auteur;
—L'oiseau, quand (((((le soleil échauffant jusqu'au marbre)))))

1. Pour qui n'a rien appris la terre est un plateau.

—The presiding judge, what points of law he's conveying
To the roof beam, while he signs a warrant or wastes his saliva talking;
—The worker who knows he has a nail in his stomach,
If he'll find it tomorrow in his chamberpot;
—The guest who's late and riskily offers a dubious excuse,
If anyone will bring back the soup tureen and ladle;
—At what price bit by bit he will sell the rope he used
To commit murder, the heir of someone found hanged;
—The hen how she managed to confuse the egg
She'd just laid with the egg of a duck;
—The ignoramus who sees a boat scud towards the open sea[1]
Until only the top fragment of its mast can still be seen,
If already its crew are fodder for sharks;
—Who are the fathers of her kids, the girl whose bed
Is never empty, such skill she displays in it;
—The lover of morphine, what rank Epicurus,
In his classification of pleasures, would have given injection;
—The mountaineer in ecstasy on the edge of a soaring range,
How to praise enough the creator of the universe;
—The bird, when (((((the sun so hot it warms even marble)))))

1. To someone who has learned nothing the earth is flat.

113　*thomas*: Slang term for chamberpot or stool, derived from the phrase, "*aller voir la mère Thomas.*"

A mountaineer admiring the view in some high place (ecstatic posture). (line 127)

En juillet on déjeune à l'ombre sous son arbre,   130
Dans quelle assiette il va, loin de se retenir,
Laisser choir en visant, tout frais, un souvenir;
—Pendant qu'il met la lune à son point, l'astronome,
S'il y va voir marcher, la tête en bas, un homme,
Telle une mouche errant au plafond à pas lents;)))),   135
Prétend déterminer son rang ou ses talents;
Pour que déféremment avec lui l'on s'exprime,
Le ferrailleur taré pose en veste d'escrime,
Comme prêt à fixer un chacun de travers;
Plume aux doigts, l'œil vers Dieu, le ciseleur de vers,   140
Qui—sans cesse y cherchant la plus millionnaire—
Des rimes sait par cœur tout le dictionnaire;
La richarde, le buste orné d'un cabochon
Digne d'une carafe en quête d'un bouchon;
En surtout d'Esquimau, le revenant du pôle,   145
Dont les mensonges sont à l'abri du contrôle;
Son violon au cou, le joueur éminent
Que dispute à l'ancien le nouveau continent;
Face à son chevalet, l'émule altier d'Apelle
Dont rayonne le nom, centre d'une chapelle;   150
Raquette au poing, sans veste, en blanc frais, sans gilet,
Le roi du tennis qui se moque du filet;

One eats outdoors in July under a shady tree,
On which plate, far from restraining itself,
It will let fall a fresh, deliberately aimed souvenir;
—While he focuses the moon in his lens, the astronomer,
If he will see a man walking upside down there,
Like a fly wandering slowly over a ceiling;)))),
Assertively presents his rank or his talents;
So that you express yourself deferentially to him,
The swashbuckler with the damaged reputation poses
In his fencing vest, as if ready to skewer anyone;
With his pen in hand, his eye aimed at God, the chiseller of verse,
Who—forever searching there for the most opulent effects—
Knows by heart his rhyming dictionary;
The very rich woman, with her bust adorned by a vast gem
Big enough for a water carafe in search of a stopper;
In his Eskimo overcoat, the explorer back from the Pole,
Whose lies can never be challenged;
His violin at his neck, the virtuoso
For whose talents the New World is competing with the Old;
Facing his easel, the haughty rival of Apelles
Whose name is a beacon, and who is the center of a clique;
Holding his racquet, without jacket or waistcoat, in fresh whites,
The king of tennis who treats the net with disdain;

136 *Prétend déterminer son rang ou ses talents*: This returns us to the syntactic unit interrupted at line 19.

149 *Apelle*: Legendary Greek painter of the 4th century BC.

An astronomer focusing a telescope. If the sky is visible (it's not indispensable this be the case), the telescope should be aimed at a full moon. (lines 133–35)

Tout équipé, l'oisif épris de vénerie,
Lançant, martiale, en selle une sonnerie;
L'argumenteur de marque, en robe, qu'au barreau   155
L'on jalouse, tant il fait chômer le bourreau;
L'arrivé pianiste au clavier, chez qui, même,
Énergique et propre au trille est le quatrième;
Tel qu'excentrique, avec l'accent d'un fils de John
Bull, sur la piste il parle à l'écuyer, le clown;   160
Le grand musicien, comme lorsqu'il compose,
Traçant tel final point d'orgue sur une pause;
Sec sous sa casaque ample à clairsemés gros pois,
Le jockey pour qui cent livres sont un gros poids;)))
Se fait prendre en famille une beauté qui, mûre,   165
N'entend plus sur ses pas monter aucun murmure,
De mère, sur la plaque, elle se change en sœur;))
L'avis roulant sur l'art de mouvoir l'ascenseur;)
—Racines, troncs, rameaux, branches collatérales—
L'état de ses aïeux; les frustes cathédrales;   170
Voire le fier menhir, l'original cromlech,
Le dolmen sous lequel le sol est toujours sec.

In full riding dress, the idler who loves hunting,
Blowing, in martial spirit, on his horn from his saddle;
In legal robes the famous barrister who's the envy of all
At the bar, because he so often gives the hangman a holiday;
At the keys the successful pianist, whose
Fourth finger produces crisp and lively trills;
Dressed in his eccentric garb, as when, adopting a John Bull accent,
He parleys with the horseman in the ring, the clown;
The great composer in the act of composition,
Writing some final fermata after a rest;
Dry under his large green polka-dot jacket,
The jockey for whom a hundred pounds is a great weight;)))
A beauty has her picture taken with her family, one who is now
    mature
And no longer hears murmurs when she passes,
On the photographic plate she changes from mother to sister;))
The notice explaining how the elevator should be operated;)
—Roots, trunks, branches, collateral branches—
The status of his ancestors; ancient cathedrals;
Even the proud menhir, the prehistoric cromlech,
And the dolmen under which the ground is always dry.

165 *Se fait prendre:* The mature woman who miraculously changes from mother to sister on the photographic plate is illustrating the power of photographic retouching hailed in line 14.

168 *L'avis roulant sur l'art de mouvoir l'ascenseur:* Because he lives at the top of his building, the photographer who is so skillful at retouching photographs is forever going up and down in the elevator, and thus knows extremely well the notice about how to operate it.

171–72 *menhir. . . cromlech . . . dolmen:* A menhir is a prehistoric standing stone, and cromlech and dolmen both denote megalithic burial chambers. Since these are normally dated to 4000 to 3000 BC, they are in fact likely to be as old as or older than many Egyptian monuments. Roussel has, however, claimed only that the crumbling marvels of Egypt *seem* to make them date from yesterday (line 7).

A man on horseback, seen from
the front, dressed for hunting and
blowing a horn. (lines 153–54)

II

Le Champ de bataille des Pyramides

Rien que de l'évoquer sur ce champ de bataille,
A l'âge où le surtout—le long surtout à taille—
Et le *petit chapeau*—desquels nous extrayons
Quel que soit notre bord d'intimidants rayons—
(Extraire à tout propos est naturel à l'homme;   5
Il extrait: de ce rien, la chute d'une pomme,
Une loi qui le voue à l'immortalité;
D'une fable ou d'un conte une moralité;
Du grêle épouvantail, simple croix qui se dresse
—Sa tenue accusant la plus noire détresse—   10
((Que d'aspects prend la croix! un groupement astral

II

The Battlefield of the Pyramids

The mere evocation of his presence on this battlefield,
At an age when the great coat—the long fitted greatcoat—
And the *little hat*—from which we deduce,
Whatever our perspective, an intimidating aura—
(To deduce at every turn is natural to man;
He deduces: from this nothing, the fall of an apple,
A law that consecrates him to immortality;
From a fable or story a moral;
From a thin scarecrow, a simple erect cross—
Its getup indicating the most dire poverty—
((How many aspects the cross assumes! A group of stars

Le Champ de bataille des Pyramides: The Battle of the Pyramids was fought at Embabeh near Cairo on July 21, 1798. Although not yet dressed in the long grey greatcoat and *little hat* that radiated such an intimidating aura, Napoleon comprehensively defeated the Mamluk forces of Mural Bey and Ibrahim Bey.

4   *d'intimidant rayons*: 633 lines, including those in footnotes, elapse before we return to Napoleon's hat and greatcoat at line 605 of the main text.

7   *Une loi*: A reference to Sir Isaac Newton's discovery of the laws of gravity.

10   *noire détresse*: The deduction to be made from the miserably and unconvincingly attired scarecrow is that of the "*foncière bêtise*" (the basic stupidity) of birds (line 604).

11   *Que d'aspects prend la croix!*: Lines 11–22 present four further examples, in addition to that of the scarecrow, of the different aspects assumed by the cross. A fifth is begun at line 31, but is almost immediately interrupted; this syntactic unit is finally picked up and completed in line 602.

A scarecrow for sparrows (a cross
dressed in an old coat and an old hat).
No people. (lines 9–10 and 603–4)

Forme celle du sud au cœur du ciel austral;
Figurément parlant, tous nous portons la nôtre;
Quand un juste succès remporté par un autre
Eut l'approbation d'un de ces envieux   15
Qui, sourdement rageurs, sans percer se font vieux,
—Cerveaux poussifs privés de toute flamme innée,—
Ses familiers en font une à la cheminée;
Sans faute, une fois l'an,—parti le carnaval,—
(((Pour peu qu'il soit du moins sur le rite à cheval   20
Et, croyant à l'enfer, redoute d'y descendre)))
Le chrétien, sur le front, s'en fait mettre une en cendre;
Quand délibérément ((((s'approcher d'un repas
Est un ravigotant sans rival pour le pas;
Quand vers le râtelier un équipage cingle,   25
Les chevaux fendent l'air sans que le fouet les cingle,
Tels des pur-sang issus d'illustres étalons;)))
On gagne un restaurant,—à l'heure où les talons
De tout bon estomac sont la place attitrée,—
Souvent, près d'un rôti, par la porte vitrée[1],   30

1. Si l'homme, pour bâtir, n'usait que de cristal
   (Tel l'intermède ami qui coupe un récital,
   Une note distrait, donne un peu d'insomnie),

Forms the Southern Cross in the heart of southern skies;
Figuratively speaking, we all bear our own;
When a deserved success achieved by another
Receives the approbation of one of those envious types
Who, raging inside, wear themselves out without a breakthrough,
—Wheezing intellects bereft of all inner spark,—
His intimates around the hearth make one;
Without fail, once a year,—after the carnival is over—
(((As long as he is at least one who keeps up with the rite,
And, believing in hell, fears descending there)))
The Christian has one put on his forehead in ashes;
When resolutely (((approaching a meal
Is an unrivalled stimulant to speed;
When a horse-and-carriage tears towards the rack in the stable,
The horses cleave the air without the lash of the whip
Like thoroughbreds born of famous stallions;)))
One enters a restaurant,—at the time of day
When all self-respecting stomachs experience pangs of hunger,—
Often, just by the roast, through a glass door[1],

1. If man, when building, used only crystal
    (Like the friendly interval which divides a recital,
    A footnote distracts, induces a little wakefulness),

19 *une fois l'an*: i.e., on Ash Wednesday. Ash from the previous year's Palm Sunday Crosses is mixed with oil of catechumens to form a paste with which the priest makes a sign of the cross on the communicants' foreheads.

A priest making a cross in ashes on the
forehead of a worshipper. (line 22)

On voit se mettre en croix (((tandis que le patron
((((Quelque spécialiste en fait de bonne chère,
Qui frémirait de voir un fruit d'espèce chère

Il frapperait à mort plus d'une calomnie
(Et le soleil, enfin, éclairerait les cours!);   5
Combien continueraient, toutefois, d'avoir cours!
Celle entre autres, hélas! qui consiste à prétendre
(Bien que, sans contredit, même en son âge tendre,
La vieille humanité n'ait jamais vu son dos)
Que la lune (ce monde où règne le repos,   10
Où nul zéphyr ne souffle, où nul volcan ne jongle,
Monde dont nous portons à la base de l'ongle
—Sans soupçonner à quoi, tel qu'il est, il nous sert—
((Mais à quoi sert le lac qui nous leurre au désert,
Nous faisant espérer la boisson et la pêche?   15
A quoi notre frisson au vu de la dépêche
Dont nous ne déchirons la bande qu'en tremblant?))
Un timide portrait réduit mais ressemblant,
Décoratif surtout présenté par le pouce,
Monde récalcitrant où nul germe ne pousse,   20
Vu qu'il n'a pas en tout, sur lui, ce qu'il faut d'eau
—Là, point de naufragé priant sur son radeau
Ni de pays portant le nom de Finistère—
Pour baptiser, pour peindre ou pour prendre un clystère;)
Agit en satellite éminemment poltron.   25

One sees put into the shape of a cross (((while the *patron*
((((Some specialist in the business of good living,
Who would tremble to see an expensive fruit

It would put to an end to many a calumny
(And the sun would finally light up courtyards!);
How many, however, would continue to have currency!
That, among others, alas, which consists of the claim
(Although, and this cannot be denied, even in its tender youth
Ancient humanity has never seen its dark side)
That the moon (this world where peace reigns,
Where no wind ever blows, where no volcano juggles rocks,
A world of which we carry at the base of the nail
—Without being able to conjecture what purpose it serves—
((But what purpose does the lake that deceives us in the desert serve,
Giving us hopes of drink and fish?
What's the point of the shiver at the sight of the telegram
Which we tear open in a fit of trembling?))
A shy, miniature, but accurate portrait,
Attractive in particular on the nail of the thumb,
A world that is rebarbative, where no seed ever grows,
On account of the fact it lacks the necessary water
—There, one finds no shipwreck victim praying on a raft
And no region bearing the name Finisterre—
To baptise, to paint, or to have an enema;)
Is an utter poltroon in its behavior as a satellite.

Footnote 1 (from previous page), line 23 *Finistère*: The tip of the Breton peninsula (literally, land's end).

31 *On voit se mettre en croix*: To find out what is being put into the shape of a cross in the restaurant, turn to line 602, and Zo's illustration, no. 40.

A woman tearing open a
telegram. Anxious expression.
(footnote 1, lines 16–17)

Subir l'attouchement d'une lame d'acier)))),
Sachant que l'homme porte, avisé besacier,   35
Dans une poche ronde à souhait qu'il croit plate,
Ses personnels défauts derrière l'omoplate
((((Dès que l'homme, au surplus, pour avoir ausculté
(((((Comme on fait d'un jeune être à qui la Faculté
A défendu l'amour et la fenêtre close   40
En le trouvant miné par la tuberculose,
Qui, dure aux jouvenceaux, respecte l'âge mûr)))))
Pendant qu'on l'épluchait telle porte ou tel mur
(((((Gardons-nous d'oublier qu'en effet la voix porte
Au delà d'un mur mince, au delà d'une porte;))))),   45
Voit tout nus ses défauts, ses tics, ses appétits,
Par ses yeux complaisants ils sont rendus petits
(((((Tels:—l'ombre, vers midi, sur le cadran solaire,
Montrant que l'estomac réclame son salaire;
—Par le gel, le niât-on, le mètre étalon;   50
—Défiant la crotte un retroussé pantalon;
—Un journal sur la planche à trou d'un édicule;
—La botte à retaper dont le talon s'écule;
—Ce qu'attentif décoiffe à coups d'ongle un rabbin;
—Lorsqu'il met le couvert la pile d'un larbin;   55
—Mû par un barbier, un dossier de fauteuil tiède;

Submit to the touch of a blade of steel)))),
Knowing that each man carries, like one prudently bearing a
    knapsack,
In a pouch which each thinks flat, but is as bulging as you like,
His personal faults behind the shoulder blades
((((As soon as, moreover, a man, having pressed his ear
(((((As they do to a young person to whom the doctors
Have forbidden both love and closed windows,
Having discovered he is being sapped by tuberculosis,
Which, cruel to young people, respects those of a mature age)))))
To some door or wall while those on the other side were criticizing
    him,
(((((Let us be careful not to forget that the voice carries
Through a thin wall or a door)))))
Sees his faults, his mannerisms, and his appetites laid bare,
By his complacent eyes they are reduced in size
(((((Just as is:—the shadow towards midday on the sundial,
Showing that the stomach can demand its reward;
—By the frost, who can deny it, the standard meter;
—Defying the mud, a rolled-up trouser leg;
—A newspaper by a wooden seat in a public toilet;
—The boot waiting to be fixed whose heel is wearing away;
—That from which the rabbi carefully removes the foreskin with flicks
    of the nail;
—While he lays the table, a flunky's pile of plates;
—Moved by a barber, the headrest of a warm barber's chair;

37   *derrière l'omoplate*: It is easy to get lost at this point in the canto. The discerning *patron* is acutely aware of human vanity. It is vanity which leads one to think the pouch in which one's faults are stored behind the shoulder blades is almost flat, and it is to this vanity that he appeals when he resurfaces at line 507, looking to add to his greeting a bit of fulsome flattery ("*cherche un coup d'encensoir joindre à son salut*"). The *patron*'s image of each of us carrying a pouch or wallet in which our faults are stored derives from La Fontaine's "La Besace" (Book 1, Fable 7), whose concluding lines are:

> *Le fabricateur souverain*
> *Nous créa besaciers tous de même manière,*
> *Tant ceux du temps passé que du temps d'aujourd'hui:*
> *Il fit pour nos défauts la poche de derrière,*
> *Et celle de devant pour les défauts d'autrui.*

> The sovereign creator
> Made us all wallet-bearers of the same kind,
> Those living in times past, and those alive today;
> He made for our own faults a pouch on our backs
> And a pouch at the front for the faults of others.

48   (((((*Tels*: A "hook" introducing 39 examples of things that have got smaller presented as analogous to the way the faults of the eavesdropper are made to shrink by his "*yeux complaisants.*" The overarching theme is still that of vanity, for it is vanity that makes the eavesdropper minimize the faults he overhears itemized through the door or wall.

50   *le mètre étalon*: From 1889 to1960 the standard meter was defined as the length of a platinum-iridium (90:10) alloy bar, which Roussel suggests will shrink in extremely cold temperatures. (*Étalon à platine* is also one of the word formations used to generate an episode of *Impressions d'Afrique* [*CJ*, p.16]). For an explanation of the *procédé* (method) Roussel used to write his novels and plays and revealed in "Comment j'ai écrit certains de mes livres," see note to line 1 of footnote beginning at line 62 of Canto IV.

52   *Un journal sur la planche*: The newspaper gets smaller as it is used for what lines 552–53 call "*certains essuyages intimes, / En aveugle accompli*" ("certain intimate wipings / Accomplished without looking").

A sundial indicating a few minutes
before midday. (line 48)

—Le mètre, au réveil, qu'un soldat ancien possède;
—Juliette, au gala d'Éjur, et Roméo
Par deux mimes enfants faits *gratis pro Deo*;
—Le fer vaincu qu'en scène un preux rompt sur sa cuisse;   60
—Le pain qu'en salivant guide à la messe un suisse;
—L'asperge au rancart mise après le coup de dent;
—Quand sert la bêche, un ver à mortel accident;
—La canne à dard demi-nu quand fausse est l'alerte;
—Le trop haut pupitre à musique fraîche ouverte;   65
—Quand pousse un pianiste enfant, son siège à vis;
—L'âgé calendrier-bloc, corpulent jadis;
—La suspension qu'on remise après la soupe;
—La bande de papier postal lorsqu'on se coupe;
—La tache attristant la glace où l'haleine a pris;   70
—Au premier éclair qui compte, la voile à ris;
—La table après un grand dîner réarrondie;
—L'arche où monte, agressive, une eau qu'on étudie;
—Au puant souffle à but du fumeur, l'amadou;
—La queue à bout neuf en sang du jeune toutou;   75
—Quand le dressage agit, l'oisif bout de gourmette;
—Quand sa tête arrive à choir, l'éteinte allumette;
—L'ouvert tube à demi plat qu'enroule un rapin;
—Quand, mûr, son bouton part, l'élastique à pépin;

—Each morning, the meter-long tape measure of a seasoned soldier;
—In the gala at Éjur, Juliet and Romeo
When played for free by two child mime actors;
—The conquered sword that a knight breaks on his thigh on the stage;
—The bread that a salivating verger distributes at mass;
—The asparagus stalk put aside after it's been bitten;
—When a spade is being used, a worm that suffers a fatal accident;
—The half-drawn swordstick when it's a false alarm;
—The just-opened music stand that is too high;
—When a child pianist grows, the piano stool;
—The ageing tear-off calendar that was once thick;
—The hanging lamp that gets raised after supper;
—The strip of letter paper when one cuts oneself;
—The melancholy stain on the mirror made by someone's breath;
—At the first threatening flash of lightning, the sail that must be
   reefed;
—After a large dinner party, the table when it's made round again;
—The arch of the bridge up which a closely watched floodwater is fast
   rising;
—The tinder when blown on by the stinking breath of a smoker;
—The bleeding, just-docked tail of a young doggie;
—When dressage is in progress, the idle end of the curb bit;
—When its head falls off, the extinguished match;
—The open, half-empty tube of paint that an art student rolls up;
—When, getting old, its button drops off, the elastic umbrella
   fastener;

57   *Le mètre, au réveil*: A reference to a ritual practiced in the French army: those nearing the end of their term of military service would count down the last hundred days by each morning snipping a centimeter off a meter-long tape measure.

58   *Juliette, au gala d'Éjur*: The first of two references in this canto to scenes from Roussel's own fiction. The gala of the Incomparables presented in Éjur in *Impressions d'Afrique* (1910) includes a performance by Kalj and Méisdehl, both aged between seven and eight, of scenes from the original, much longer—and much weirder—script of *Romeo and Juliet* that the tragedian Adinolfa discovered in a secret compartment in the country house she purchased from Lord Dewsbury on the banks of the Thames (see chapters 7 and 12 of *Impressions d'Afrique*). Adinolfa teaches these two Ponukéléan children a few phrases in French, but they mainly use mime to present this extraordinary additional material.

A smoker blowing on tinder
to ignite it. (line 74)

—Quand le lit prend sa place au berceau, la ruelle;   80
—Le pissenlit qu'exprès l'haleine atteint, cruelle;
—Ses pointes faites, la ballerine à clinquant;
—L'acte interprété par maître X . . . d'un délinquant;
—Quand l'arroseur cède à la soif, le jet de lance;
—Le fil qui par l'aragne escaladé balance;   85
—Au bord d'un tapis vert un honnête magot;
—Un cigare réduit à l'état de mégot;
—Le disque du soleil dans le ciel de Neptune;))))),
Comme si, choisissant la seconde opportune,
Un ensorcellement eût su le rendre enclin   90
A prendre:—l'appareil qui, trouvé par Franklin,
Sans danger dans un puits fait se perdre la foudre
Pour un fil gris passé dans une aiguille à coudre;
—Pour ceux dont s'orne un bras arrivé d'officier
Au ciel trois jumeaux blancs astres d'artificier;   95
—Quand, médian, le coupe un trait, pour la bavette
D'un prêtre, un tableau noir;—l'empli tube à cuvette
D'un chaud thermomètre à bientôt peter réduit,
Pour une épingle à chef rond;—la laisse que suit,
Tiède, un collier veuf du chien qui de près lui touche,   100
Pour un fil d'ombrelle à cercle;—une spire à douche
A système accompli, pour un naïf ressort

When the bed replaces the cradle, the gap between bedside and wall;
—The dandelion that someone deliberately, cruelly, blows upon;
—Having finished being *en pointe*, the tinselled ballerina;
—The act of a delinquent as interpreted by barrister X . . . ;
—When the waterer gives in to thirst, the spray from the hose;
—The thread that dangles after the spider has climbed it;
—On the edge of a gaming table, a fair-sized pile of money;
—A cigar reduced to a butt;
—The disc of the sun as seen in Neptune's sky;))))),
As if, choosing exactly the right moment,
Some sorcery had succeeded in making him inclined
To mistake:—the apparatus that, discovered by Franklin,
Makes lightning disappear harmlessly into a pit,
For a grey thread passed through the eye of a needle;
—For those with which the arm of a military officer is adorned,
The three adjacent white stars in the sky created by a maker of
    fireworks;
—A blackboard, when a line cuts it in half down the middle,
For the bib of a priest;—the filled tube and bulb
Of a thermometer so heated it's about to burst,
For a pin with a round head;—the leash from which
Hangs a warm empty dog collar, for the strap
Of an umbrella with a circular fastener;—a radial shower
With a sophisticated water system, for a simple

88   *le ciel de Neptune*: Since Neptune is further from the sun than the earth, the sun's disc would look smaller when seen in Neptune's skies than it does when seen in earth's.

89–91   These lines pick up from lines 46–47: it is as if the eavesdropper has fallen under a spell that makes him inclined to mistake big things for little things. There follow 207 examples that occupy 416 lines (91–506). In each case the item introduced by "*pour*" (or "for") is the smaller. This is by far the longest list in the poem.

101   *une spire à douche*: Jean Ferry observes: "It's a question here of those shower systems that operate not through an overhead shower rose, but by means of a tube which, spiraling down around a cylindrical generator, washes the body from head to foot. It is this kind of shower, one no doubt rare and expensive, that Roussel, describing it as '*accompli*,' opposes to the small coil-spring such as one finds in a cheap lighter, and which he felicitously describes as '*naïf*'" (*UE*, pp. 67–68).

A barrister pleading a case.
Vehement posture. (line 83)

A boudin;—l'éteignoir fidèle au cierge mort,
Pour ce qui taille un blanc crayon noir d'ingénue
A carnet de bal;—la boule aquatique et nue   105
D'un dentaire effrayant recoin, pour l'abreuvoir
D'un serin sobre;—pour l'arrière, à son devoir
Soustrait, qu'un flot soulève, un moulin mal à l'aise
Qu'en brutal favorise un ouragan;—l'anglaise
Clé, de l'écrou gardant mémoire, pour un quart   110
De soupir;—pour un œuf au plat seul à l'écart,
Salé ferme à son centre, un baissé crâne à rite
D'âgé prêtre à jaunisse; et pour la marguerite
Sans tige où rien n'accuse un revers à tronçon,
L'œuf au plat;—pour trois traits chics rayant sans façon   115
D'un glacé gant du soir la blancheur magnifique,
Trois touches noires sœurs;—un pied photographique,
Quand part le Rayon Vert, pour un jeté restant
De cerise triple;—en passant, pour l'attristant
Jet d'eau qu'un coude à trou lorsqu'on arrose engendre,   120
Celui d'un parc;—pour un hamac à se détendre,
Au cirque, un bissecteur filet de sûreté;
—La flèche ignare à bail sublunaire écourté
Qu'on sort d'un cœur, pour une instruite plume d'oie
A rouge encre;—un marin projecteur qui s'octroie   125

Coil-spring;—the snuffer loyally joined to the extinguished candle,
For that which sharpens the white black-leaded pencil of an ingénue
Filling in her dance card;—the free-floating watery ball
Of a frightening nook depicted with teeth, for the drinking receptacle
Of an abstemious canary;—for the rear propeller withdrawn
From its duty in the water by a wave lifting the boat, a disturbed
    windmill
That a hurricane is brutally favoring with its attentions;—the monkey
Wrench still in the shape in which it last held a screw nut, for a semi-
Quaver rest;—for a single fried egg, on its own,
With a vigorously salted yolk, the skull, bent in prayer,
Of an old priest with jaundice; and for the stemless daisy
Which has no suggestion of a stump on its underside,
A fried egg;—for three stylish lines striping
The magnificent whiteness of a glacé kid evening glove,
Three adjoining black piano keys;—a photographer's tripod,
Just as the Green Ray vanishes, for the discarded remains
Of a triple cherry;—for the dispiriting jet of water
That springs from a leaky bend in a hosepipe when one is watering,
A fountain in a park; for a hammock in which to relax,
A bisecting safety net at the circus;
—The ignorant arrow, its temporary flight beneath the moon cut
    short,
Which someone is extracting from a heart, for a learnèd goose quill
In red ink;—a marine searchlight which has the right

105　*la boule aquatique et nue*: The reference here is to chapter 2 of Roussel's *Locus Solus* (1914), in which the inventor Martial Canterel displays to his invited guests a mosaic made out of human teeth. One of the stories the mosaic presents is a scene from a Scandinavian fairy tale called "The Tale of the Watery Globe," which narrates the pursuit by eleven evil brothers of their virtuous sister Ulfra. Ulfra has been changed into a dove and is protected by an aerial globe of water; anyone touched by the globe's shadow instantly dies. The brothers are led to Ulfra's hideaway by a linnet. The bird becomes so tired it hops rather than flies, and when it passes under the shadow of the watery globe it immediately drops dead. The linnet with the globe above it is larger than, but visually similar to, an abstemious canary in its cage with its spherical transparent drinking receptacle ("*abreuvoir*") still full of water.

118　*Le Rayon Vert*: The Green Ray is an optical phenomenon that occurs just before sunset or just after sunrise; a green ray becomes visible above the sun for a few seconds. Roussel would no doubt have learned about the *Rayon Vert* from Jules Verne's 1882 novel of that name.

123　*à bail sublunaire écourté*: literally, its sublunar lease cut short. The comparison here is of an arrow whose flight has been interrupted by striking a red heart from which it is being withdrawn, and a writing quill being taken out of an inkwell containing red ink.

A fountain in a park. No
people. (lines 120–21)

Des droits de balaiement systématique, pour
Un porté falot sourd;—le jet de lest qu'au jour
Met l'aérostier qui part, pour l'interne chute
D'un sablier;—pour un rouleau clos qui débute
Comme ex-bobine à neuf ruban, un poussiéreux   130
Tambour après l'étape;—un divorcé gant creux
De cardinal, pour la massive main de marque
En corail d'où naît du bonheur;—dans une barque,
Pour deux spatules à l'usage d'un potard,
La paire d'avirons;—le nœud dont, tôt ou tard,   135
D'une fille d'Alsace à ravir le chef s'orne,
Pour un nœud lavallière à cou;—pour une borne
Près d'un banc, un menhir d'un dolmen peu distant;
—Un groupe au pas d'agents, pour l'essaim contristant
D'internes sans foyer qu'aux jours de fête on croise;   140
—Pour un pauvre O d'aphone éclos sur une ardoise,
Un cercle en un seul coup fait sur un tableau noir;
—Pour celui dont se coiffe un goulot, l'entonnoir
Avec quoi, d'un café, traçant des huit sans nombre,
On mouille la terrasse;—aux heures de pénombre,   145
Sous les tropiques, pour une chauve-souris,
Un vampire;—la carte où, chassant nos souris,
D'un mort nous dit merci la famille, pour celle

To cast its beam in a systematic, sweeping manner, for
A handheld dark lantern;—the ballast being cast overboard at
     daybreak
By the departing balloonist, for the internal fall
Of sand in an hourglass;—for a finished reel which begins life
As an ex-dispenser of new ribbon, a dusty
Drum after a day's march;—the single empty glove
Of a cardinal, for the solid, famous hand of Fatima,
Carved in coral, from which springs happiness;—in a boat,
For two spatulas being used by a chemist,
A pair of oars;—the knot with which, sooner or later,
The head of a girl from Alsace is ravishingly adorned,
For a loosely tied knot in a necktie;—for a milestone
Next to a bench, a menhir near a dolmen;
—A group of policemen walking in step, for the doleful swarm
Of homeless boarders that one meets on festival days;
—For the simple O that a mute manages to draw on a slate,
A circle made in a single go on a blackboard;
—For the dispenser that goes on top of a bottle, the funnel of the hose
With which, tracing numerous figures of eight, a cafe's
Terrace is watered;—at dusk
In the tropics, for a bat,
A vampire;—the card with which, wiping the smiles off our faces,
The family of a dead person thanks us, for that

132 *la massive main de marque*: Roussel is referring here to the *hamsa* or the hand of Fatima, a symbol of good luck. A red, empty cardinal's glove is bigger than a solid ("*massive*") hand of Fatima made of red coral, and carried or worn as a good luck charm.

A man at night carrying a lighted dark lantern. (line 127)

D'un visiteur en deuil frais;—pour de la ficelle
A sacs de confiseur coté, du cordon d'or   150
Pour képis d'officier;—dans certain corridor,
Pour deux chevrons pointe en bas proche un esprit rude,
La marque d'huis du fond;—pour une pêche où, prude,
Le regard n'ose atteindre, un rouge arrière-train
D'enfant fautif fouetté;—pour la chaînette à grain   155
Restant d'un chapelet rompu, la chaîne à boule
D'un forçat du vieux temps;—pour celle qu'à l'ampoule
L'épingle arrache à point, la fuite qu'au désert
Le fer d'un traître extorque à l'outre;—quand, disert,
Le vent rage, un radeau mâté dans une trombe,   160
Pour un toton;—signal rouge, une fiche en rhombe
De fiole à poison, pour un central débris
D'as de carreau;—pour celle à quoi, de chic épris,
Le myope, en peinant, fait s'unir son orbite,
Une glace à hublot;—pour l'averse subite   165
D'un arrosoir à fleurs, ce qui sur le chef pleut
D'une pomme à doucher;—quand, sans sauve-qui-peut,
A l'épreuve on le met, pour deux baissers de trappe,
Ceux du rideau de fer;—pour la règle qui frappe,
Quand s'en mêlent les nerfs, des doigts nus d'écolier,   170
Une poutre à décor funéraire;—un collier

Of a visitor newly in mourning;—for the twine
Around the bags of a highly esteemed confectioner, the gold braid
On the képis of officers;—at the end of a certain passage,
For two V shapes next to a Greek rough breathing,
The sign on the toilet door;—for a peach which a prudish
Person does not look at, the red backside
Of a naughty child who's been whipped;—for the small chain with a
    single bead
Left on it of a broken rosary, the ball and chain
Of a long-term convict;—for the water from a blister
That a pin draws out through a hole, the water running away in the
    desert
Released by the sword of a traitor from a water-skin;—when the gale
Rages eloquently, a masted raft in a whirlwind,
For a spinning top;—the red rhomboid marker
On a phial of poison, for the cut-out middle
Of the ace of diamonds;—for that which, in love with fashion,
The myopic painfully forces into his eye socket,
A porthole;—for the sudden downpour
From a watering can used for flowers, that which rains on the head
From a shower attachment;—when, without prompting a stampede,
Safety tests are run, for two lowerings of a trap door,
Two lowerings of a fire curtain;—for the ruler that strikes,
The nerves all a-jangle, the naked fingers of a schoolboy,
A wooden beam in a funeral scene;—the collar

152   *Pour deux chevrons pointe en bas*: Two small v shapes pointing down, if they overlap, would create a w, and if they were followed by a Greek *dasia* or rough breathing diacritical, which resembles a c, would form a miniature version of the sign on the door at the end of a certain corridor, i.e., WC.

A water-skin in the desert, from which
water is escaping through a hole
seemingly made on purpose by the
sword of a traitor. No people. (line 159)

De pilori, pour des menottes, en spectacle
Ne s'offrant qu'à demi;—pour ce qui d'un obstacle
Borde un gazon, un plant télégraphique à fil
Solitaire;—quand jacte en l'air un pitre vil,   175
Sa grosse caisse, au bord, pour un tambour de basque
Plaqué contre un miroir;—quand sur eux, sans bourrasque,
Il s'est mis à neiger, des œufs rouges massés,
Pour des fraises qu'on sucre;—en mai, temps noirs passés,
Une épousée, en plein lieu saint, pour une unique   180
Communiante;—pour le faire-part cynique
Qui par clichés procède, un journal noir de bords
A directeur défunt;—pour ce qu'ivre d'accords,
Sa main rythmant son pas, l'Espagnol fait s'ébattre,
Un claquoir;—pour l'engin d'un chef qui d'un deux-quatre   185
Multiplierait les bis, par gros temps un beaupré
D'esquif ancré;—pour la carte appelant au pré
L'insulteur, le mural rectangle mortuaire,
Marbre blanc à nom noir;—lorsque en plein sanctuaire
Bruit l'élévation, pour celle d'un laïc   190
L'hostie en jeu;—quand loin des problèmes à hic,
Son temps fait, il végète, un rogaton de craie,
Pour un sain comprimé;—pour la gemme qui raie
Le carreau vierge auquel s'attaque un vitrier,

Of a pillory, for a pair of handcuffs, of which
Only half can be seen;—for that which restricts access
Around the edge of a lawn, a telegraph pole
With only one wire;—when a vile clown blabs away,
His bass drum, on its side, for a tambourine
Placed flat against a mirror;—when there's not a gust of wind
And snow is falling, a heap of red eggs,
For strawberries being sugared;—in May, gloomy weather over,
A bride getting married in the holiest of places, for a solitary
New communicant;—for the cynical announcement of a death
Made up entirely of clichés, a newspaper with black borders
    commemorating
The paper's deceased owner;—for that which, drunk on the chords,
Her hand matching the rhythm of her steps, a Spanish dancer clacks,
An ecclesiastical wooden clapper;—for the baton of a conductor who
    multiplies
The repetition of two beats in a bar, the bowsprit in stormy weather
Of an anchored skiff;—for a card summoning to a duel in a field
The insulter, a rectangular funerary plaque
Of white marble, with the name in black;—when in the chancel
The elevation of the host is murmured, for the morsel received by a
    layperson,
The holy wafer as it goes round;—when, far from problems full of
    snags,
It merely vegetates, its time over, the stub of a piece of chalk,
For a health pill;—for the gem which scratches
The uncut pane of glass a glazier attacks,

174–75 *un plant télégraphique à fil / Solitaire*: As Jean Ferry points out, a telegraph pole with only one line is not a common sight.

185 *un claquoir*: A clapper made of two wooden boards joined by a hinge and used in religious institutions to regulate the movements of such as choristers or monks.

A man presenting his card to another. Aggressive attitudes, making one think of a duel. (lines 187–88)

Le Sancy;—l'instrument qu'en rêve un meurtrier   195
Voit prêt à l'accourcir, pour un coupe-cigares;
—Signe au quadruple aspect, la croix qui, dans les gares,
Sur les disques tournants trône, œuvre de leurs rails,
Pour un dièse;—au cirque, un groupe à hauts poitrails
D'altiers chevaux longtemps cabrés, pour une horde   200
D'hippocampes sans but;—son vol pris, pour la corde
D'un gibet prêt, quand joue avec elle un grand vent,
Un lasso;—dans le cas, équivoque souvent,
Où ses aiguilles font diamètre, une montre,
Pour un cadran à pouls;—pour le gant à rencontre   205
Volant vers un quidam, celui qui drogue en l'air
Comme enseigne;—le croc, par la grue au but clair
Vers un fleuve abaissé, pour un fer sans amorce
D'écervelé pêcheur;—l'annexe qui, de force
Mise à son chevalet, rend sourd un violon,   210
Pour une *petite m*;—dans un parc de colon,
Quelque intrus caïman proche un parasol fixe,
Pour un lézard contre un cèpe;—au cours d'une rixe,
Un brun chicot craché, pour un pépin de grain
D'un coup de langue exclu;—pour le goinfre à refrain   215
Qu'à force d'applaudir on prend, le cousin braque
Qui fonce en plein plafond;—dans un tir de baraque,

The Sancy Diamond;—the device that in dreams a murderer
Sees ready to make him a little shorter, for a cigar cutter;
—The sign made of four lines laid crosswise to indicate
Railway track that in stations sits enthroned on a turning wheel,
For a sharp in music;—at the circus, a group of proud horses
Rearing for a long time and keeping their chests high, for a horde
Of drifting seahorses;—when it's in mid-flight, for the rope
Of a waiting gallows being toyed with by a strong wind,
A lasso;—a watch whose hands are diametrically
Aligned, and therefore ambiguous, for the dial
Of an instrument used to take one's pulse;—for the glove
Sent flying in insult towards whomever, one that hangs in air
As a shop sign;—the hook, its target clear, formed by the talons of a
    crane
Lowered towards a river, for the unbaited fishhook
Of an absent-minded fisherman;—the accessory which, forcibly
Placed on the bridge of a violin, makes it mute,
For a little *m*;—in a colonial park,
An intrusive cayman near a fixed sun-umbrella,
For a lizard by a mushroom;—in the course of a scuffle,
A brown spat-out stump of a tooth, for a grape pip
Emitted with a flick of the tongue;—for the persistently guzzling
    mosquito
Whom one kills with a clap of the hands, the crazy daddy longlegs
Who speeds about up by the ceiling;—in a shooting gallery at a fair,

195   *Le Sancy*: The Sancy Diamond was purchased in 1570 in Constantinople by Nicholas Harlei, Seigneur de Sancy. Later owners included James I, Louis XIV, and Nancy Astor. It is now in the Louvre.

195   *l'instrument qu'en rêve*: i.e., the guillotine.

A violinist playing, with the mute put
on. (lines 209–10)

Pour une épingle à perle infidèle à son nœud,
Le jet d'eau qu'orne un œuf;—lorsqu'un faubourg s'émeut
Où passe un régiment, pour un jonc chic à pomme,   220
La canne en l'air sautant;—pour l'échelle où s'assomme
La rainette à bocal, celle dont sans périr
Use un scaphandre;—pour un cachet à guérir,
Une paire à mets chaud d'assiettes attractives
Formant bloc bords à bords;—quand, bras nus, mains actives,   225
Trime un faiseur de tours, son jeu subtil d'anneaux,
Pour un stock neuf de ronds à clés;—roi des tonneaux,
Le joyau d'Heidelberg, pour une tirelire;
—Pour le cachet qui tape, y mettant de quoi lire,
Des lacs de cire à lettre, une hie au travail;   230
—Pour le trou qu'un poussin fait quand finit son bail,
Celui que laisse au disque en papier l'écuyère;
—Chez un sculpteur, pour un Poucet par la bruyère
Semant droit ses cailloux, un sauf Deucalion
Jetant ses pierres;—quand, touché, grince un lion,   235
Le fusil du chasseur, pour un revolver juste
Criblant un brun caniche enragé;—pour un buste
Au socle absent, ce qu'un sable ensevelisseur
A nu laissa du Sphinx;—le jour du blanchisseur,
Un drap qu'ont de leur pourpre enrichi des menstrues,   240

For a pearl-headed tiepin disloyally separated from its knot,
A jet of water on which an egg ornamentally balances;—when a
district
Gets excited because a regiment is passing, for a walking stick with a
fancy head,
The regimental cane being thrown into the air;—for the ladder on
which
A pet tree frog in a goldfish bowl bores itself to death, that which
A man in a diving suit safely uses;—for an aspirin,
A pair of attractive plates containing hot food, one placed
Upside down exactly on top of the other;—when, with naked arms
but active hands,
The juggler toils away, his subtle set of rings
For a new stock of key rings;—king of barrels,
The jewel of Heidelberg, for a money-box;
—For the seal that strikes, creating something to read
In lakes of sealing wax, a pile-driver at work;
—For the hole which a chick makes when its lease on its egg runs out,
That which the horseback rider leaves in the paper target;
—At a sculptor's, for a Tom Thumb on the heath
Sowing his pebbles in a straight line, an unharmed Deucalion
Throwing his stones;—when, hit, a lion gnashes its teeth,
The rifle of the hunter, for a revolver justifiably
Riddling with bullets a mad brown poodle;—for a bust
Without a plinth, that which the enveloping sand
Has left bare of the Sphinx;—on laundry day,
A sheet that menstrual discharges have enriched with their purple,

228   *Le joyau d'Heidelberg*: The Heidelberg Tun is a vast wine vat held in the cellars of Heidelberg Castle. It was made in 1751, and can hold 220,000 liters of wine. It is mentioned in Jules Verne's *Cinq semaines en ballon* (1863).

233, 234   *Poucet / Deucalion*: A comparison between two sculptures. One is of Tom Thumb dropping pebbles so as to be able to find his way home in the Perrault fairy tale; the other is of Deucalion, the ancient Greek mythological figure, who was instructed to repopulate the earth after a devastating flood sent by Zeus, from which he and his wife, Pyrrha, alone were saved. Deucalion and Pyrrha were advised by the Oracle of Themis to throw stones over their backs, and these stones turned into people (see Ovid's *Metamorphoses,* Book I, lines 313–415).

A man putting a coin in a money-box
in the shape of a barrel. (line 228)

Pour un mouchoir à sang nasal;—aux coins des rues,
La plaque bleue à nom pur, pour celle où se lit
Le chiffre de maison;—pour celle où suinte au lit
Un bouquet de cheveux, la papillote grâsse
A côtelette;—pour l'ex-bascule à disgrace   245
D'un prometteur piège à rats, un loyal tremplin;
—Un tunnel, quand, vorace, il est de vapeur plein,
Pour un triste auditif conduit à tampon d'ouate;
—Pour un dé, gaine-annexe au tiers doigt adéquate,
Lorsqu'il pose à l'envers, le gobelet à tours;   250
—Pour celui des croupiers, si pur soit-il toujours
De rouge caoutchouc, le sourd racloir à boue;
—Le jeu qui semble au chien fait pour qu'on le rabroue,
Pour un groupe au rancart, par les noirs pris aux blancs,
D'obscurs pions d'échecs;—quand, de l'eau plein ses flancs, 255
Presque enfonce un canot, ce qui part des écopes,
Pour d'humains postillons;—un toit pour télescopes,
Pour l'un, de l'autre veuf, des hémisphères forts
De Magdebourg;—l'enfant, fruit d'occultes rapports,
Sur tel voyant rond-point mis, pour l'émergeant hôte   260
D'une galette à faire un roi;—quand côte à côte
S'emballent deux chevaux, leur timon enchaîné,
Pour une flèche au vol bas;—pour un dégainé

For a handkerchief stained by nasal blood;—on the corner of streets,
The blue plaque commemorating a hallowed name, for that inscribed
With the number of a house;—for the curl paper in which bunched
    hair
Sweats in bed, the grease paper wrapping up
A cutlet;—for the ex-see-saw, which has led to the rodent's disgrace,
Of an inviting rat trap, a trustworthy springboard;
—A voracious tunnel when it's gorged itself on steam,
For a sad ear canal wadded with cotton wool;
—For a thimble, just big enough to fit on one's middle finger,
A magician's trick goblet, when he turns it the wrong way up;
—For that used by croupiers, so unsullied it's made always
Of red rubber, a dull, mud-spattered rake;
—Skittles in the game that seems to the dog designed so he's scolded,
For a group of white pawns, taken by black pieces,
Set aside during a chess match;—when, full to the gunwales with
    water,
A dinghy almost sinks, that which leaves the balers,
For humans' splutter;—a roof made especially for telescopes,
For the top half of one of the strong Magdeburg
Hemispheres;—the child, the fruit of a secret affair,
Who's abandoned on some conspicuous roundabout, for the figurine
Who emerges from a *galette à faire un roi*;—when, side by side,
Two horses bolt, the shaft to which they're both chained,
For a low-flying arrow;—for an unsheathed

253 *le jeu qui semble au chien fait pour qu'on le rabroue*: A periphrastic way of referring to the game of bowling known as skittles. Roussel is suggesting that dogs often knock over skittles while a game is in progress, and this results in these dogs being told off by the disgruntled players. These skittles are larger than, but visually similar to, a group of white pawns taken and set aside in a group together in the course of a chess match.

258–59 *des hémisphères forts / De Magdebourg*: The comparison here is between the dome of a planetary observatory and the upper hemisphere of the Magdeburg hemispheres. The latter were designed by Otto von Guericke, a German scientist, and mayor of Magdeburg, to illustrate the concept of a vacuum. The two copper hemispheres, whose rims matched exactly, were fitted together, sealed, and the air pumped out of them, after which not even teams of horses could pull them apart.

260–61 *l'émergeant hôte / D'une galette à faire un roi*: A reference to cakes, traditionally eaten around the time of Epiphany, in which a bean was secreted; whoever received the bean was king for a day, and allowed to wear a gold cardboard crown. In the latter half of the 19th century, beans were replaced by porcelain figurines, and it is one of these that, emerging from the cake, offers a visual analogy to the child abandoned on a conspicuous traffic roundabout.

A gaming table on which a croupier's rake is lying. No people. (lines 251–52)

Cuir à rasoir, la carte à commander qu'encadre
Un rectangle à poignée;—un brûle-bout de ladre,   265
Pour un plat clou-punaise en solitaire exil
La pointe en l'air;—en Suisse, au bazar, pour un cil,
Courbe évadé d'un œil doux, une corne noire
De chamois;—à son clou mise, une bassinoire,
Pour un balancier mort, à revivre appelé;   270
—Dans un char à bras en état d'être attelé,
L'avilissant harnais d'homme, pour des bretelles;
—Chez l'impure, un suave oreiller à dentelles,
Pour la pelote où rit, de trous vierge, un volant;
—Posé par l'escrimeur las, un masque isolant,   275
Pour un protège-orbite à remettre aux lunettes
D'un casseur de cailloux;—la tempe aux rides nettes
D'un vieux, pour le revers supérieur d'un poing;
—Pour le décoiffant drap noir d'un metteur au point,
Celui dont, faisant du vent, à quatre on recouvre   280
Un cercueil;—l'album à gens, s'il faut pour qu'il s'ouvre
Vaincre un ou deux fermoirs, pour un paroissien;
—Pour un tire-bouton vil, le croc quasi sien
Qui, sort noble, aux cinq doigts chez le manchot supplée;
—L'écharpe à mettre un bras, pour celle où, décuplée,   285
S'est cloîtrée une joue un jour de fluxion;

Razor strop, a restaurant menu in a rectangular
Frame to be held in the fist;—the candle end of a miser,
For a flat-headed thumbtack on its own
With its point in the air;—in Switzerland, at the bazaar, for an eyelash,
Curved escapee from a soft eye, the black horn
Of a chamois;—a warming pan after it's been hung on its nail,
For a motionless pendulum, called back to life;
—In a rickshaw just as it's being readied,
The puller's degrading harness, for a pair of braces;
—At a lewd woman's house, a pleasant lace-fringed pillow,
For an unused pincushion with a merry flounce;
—A mask put aside by a tired fencer,
For an eye protector to be placed over the glasses
Of a stonebreaker;—the clearly wrinkled temple
Of an old man, for the upper part of the underside of a fist;
—For the hair-tousling black cloth of a photographer,
That with which, generating a breeze, four people cover
A coffin;—an album of portraits, if, to open it,
You have to overcome one or two fasteners, for a prayer-book;
—For a lowly buttonhook, the hook, almost a part of his body,
Whose noble fate is to stand in for the five fingers of an armless man;
—An arm sling, for the scarf in which a much enlarged
Cheek is hidden on a day when it's inflamed;

A man with his arm in a sling—the
sling pretty wide. (line 285)

—Lorsqu'il rend le fer chaud mûr pour la flexion,
Pour un excitateur d'âtre, un soufflet de forge;
—Pour ce qu'un tousseur montre au docteur pour la gorge,
Un cavernaire arceau, par le couchant rougi,   290
A stalactite unique;—un lac de sang surgi
Dans un quartier suspect, pour le crachat perfide
D'un phtisique;—chez un sellier, l'attache où, vide,
Miroite un étrier, pour un feu ceinturon
D'ombrelle jaune;—pour le grain traître à juron   295
Qu'un mangeur de gibier, de côté, crache au diable,
Un boulet fendant l'air;—lorsque irrémédiable
L'inondation s'y frotte, un carton à tir,
Pour le domino « double as »;—le voyant partir,
Pour un bouchon sauteur qu'on lâche, un cylindrique   300
Ascenseur;—pour le dard frêle où le nord s'indique,
Une ligne d'absent qui flotte et coupe en deux
Un bassin;—sentinelle au poste hasardeux,
Au tir, sur son fond blanc, pour une ombre chinoise,
La silhouette noire;—une paire sournoise   305
De bolas, droit au but volant câble tendu,
Pour un haltère;—quand l'escrimeur s'est fendu,
Pour une serpe, son fleuret fier d'être courbe;
—Pour la gueule, au tonneau, gobant, sans nulle fourbe,

—When he's making iron hot enough to be bent,
For a pair of hearth bellows, the bellows used in a forge;
—For that which someone with a cough shows to a throat doctor,
An arched cavern, reddened by the setting sun,
With a solitary stalactite;—a lake of blood that appears
In a dangerous district, for the treacherous spittle
Of a consumptive;—at a saddler's, the tether
From which an empty stirrup gleams, for the broken fastener
Of a yellow umbrella;—for the perfidious, sworn-at bit of shot
That an eater of game spits aside, cursing it to the devil,
A cannonball cleaving the air;—when it cannot be saved,
Having been caught up in a flood, a shooting target,
For a double-one domino;—as one watches it begin to rise,
For a leaping cork released from its bottle, a cylindrical
Lift;—for the trembling compass needle that indicates north,
The line of an invisible fisherman that quivers and cuts in half
A reservoir;—a sentry at a dangerous post,
In firing position against a white background, for, at a pantomime
    shadow play,
A black silhouette;—a pair of cunningly thrown
Bolas, flying straight at their target, the cable between them fully
    stretched,
For a dumbbell;—when a fencer has lunged,
For a billhook, his foil that is proud to be bent into a curve;
—For the mouth, in *jeu de tonneau*, that swallows, without cheating,

289 *Pour ce qu'un tousseur montre au docteur pour la gorge*: i.e., an inflamed uvula.

Two domino players, one of whom
has in his fingers, ready to play it, the
double one. (line 299)

Un palet bien lancé, celle où choit du corbeau   310
Le fromage;—le pli chargé dont tout est beau,
Lorsqu'il pose, excentrique, adresse contre table,
Pour un cinq rouge;—pour le trident intraitable
Qui monte l'huître au bec, celui qui, du dehors,
Hisse au grenier le foin;—quand devant deux décors   315
Qu'un mur sépare il tombe, un sec rideau de nues,
Pour un voile abaissé sur un nez fin;—quand, nues,
Elles se croisent, pour des ciseaux trop ouverts,
Deux lames libres;—quand sont clos ses volets verts,
Un blanc bloc de maisons dans une rue en pente,   320
Pour du roquefort;—un gazon courbe où serpente
Un tuyau d'eau, pour une épaule d'immortel
Où rampe un cheveu long;—pour un couloir d'hôtel
A numéros de clés lourds, un boulevard riche,
Plein d'enseignes à tige;—aveugle ému qui triche,   325
Pour l'enfant qu'un bandeau sangle au colin-maillard,
Un mûr parlementaire;—aux halles, quand, gaillard,
Il rôde à son abri, pour celui du saint-père,
Le blanc chapeau d'un fort;—un fauve sein prospère
De nourrice en vert clair, pour un marron qui point,   330
Fendant son contenant;—lorsque à brûle-pourpoint
Il se retourne, pour une coupe trop pleine,

A well-aimed disc, that into which falls the crow's
Cheese;—the stamp on the back of a registered envelope that's fine
In every respect, when it's placed, eccentrically, with its address against
    the table,
For a red five in cards;—for the unmanageable three-pronged fork
Which lifts an oyster mouthwards, that which hoists hay
Into the hayloft from outside;—when it falls in front of two stage
    backdrops
Separated by a wall, a thin curtain depicting clouds,
For a veil being lowered over a thin nose;—when, unsheathed,
Two independent knife blades cross, for a pair
Of wide-open scissors;—when its green shutters are closed,
A white block of houses on a steep road,
For a roquefort cheese;—a curved lawn across which snakes
A hosepipe, for the shoulder of an immortal member of the *Académie
    française*
On which a long hair trails;—for the corridor of a hotel
With its heavy numbered keys in the doors, a rich boulevard
Full of heavy shop signs;—blindfolded, excited, cheating,
For the child made to wear a bandage when playing blind man's buff,
A mature peace emissary;—at the market, when, cheery,
He prowls around under the shelter it affords, for that of the Pope,
The white hat of a strong porter;—the tanned healthy breast
Of a wet nurse dressed in bright green, for a ripe chestnut
Splitting open its outer layers;—when it turns itself
Inside out, for a cup that is too full,

310–11 *où choit du corbeau / Le fromage*: A reference to the Aesop fable, "The Fox and the Crow," in which the crow drops the piece of cheese it holds in its beak, after a flattering fox has persuaded it to sing.

322 *une épaule d'immortel*: Members of the *Académie française* wear "*un habit vert*" for the institution's ceremonies.

An emissary with his eyes blindfolded (an officer) led by two soldiers wearing uniforms different from his. No other people. (line 327)

Un rouge parapluie;—assidue à la peine,
Pour celle qu'un chanceux fait trimer au tonneau,
La roue à bain froid d'un moulin;—un blanc panneau   335
Qu'un porte-riflards plein pare, asile à cinq places,
Pour du neuf papier à chant;—pour l'une des glaces
Qui, des dents, servent, monstre, au dentiste un reflet,
Un miroir concave à barbe;—pour le sifflet
Qu'est la bouche aux index livrée, un jeu de grâces   340
Avant l'envol du rond;—pour l'os aux branches grasses
Qu'un jour faste à poulet, pour rire, à deux l'on rompt,
Un éperon poudreux;—pour deux pleurs au vol prompt,
Ce qu'expulse un grippé d'espèce malapprise
Qui dans ses doigts se mouche;—un jour exempt de brise,   345
Pour un vide encrier, qu'on repaît d'encre, un seau
Qui d'asphalte s'emplit;—lorsqu'il fait d'un vaisseau
Signe, armé de rouge, un bras, pour une allumette
Dure à tuer;—pour ceux qu'avant qu'on le remette
Montre un bouchon, des mots gravés dans un tronçon   350
D'arbre scié;—quand du coude seul, sans façon,
Contre un mur il s'appuie, un bras nu de poseuse,
Pour un index frappeur;—lorsqu'une mère, oseuse,
Ouvre un berceau, les blancs rideaux, pour deux feuillets
Non coupés qu'on disjoint;—zigzaguant sans œillets,   355

A red umbrella;—assiduous in performing its painful task,
For that set in motion by someone playing *jeu de tonneau*,
The wheel of a water-mill in its cold bath;—a white panel
That is adorned by an umbrella holder containing five umbrellas,
For new music paper;—for one of those mirrors
That gives a monstrously enlarged reflection of teeth to a dentist,
The concave mirror of a barber;—for a whistler
Whistling with both index fingers in the mouth, a game of *grâces*
Before the first ring is thrown;—for the bone, with its greasy branches,
That a couple, some auspicious day when they have chicken, break in
    half, laughing,
A dusty spur;—for two tears that fall quickly,
That which is expelled by a badly brought up influenza-sufferer,
Who uses his fingers for a handkerchief;—on a day free from wind,
For an empty inkwell that is being replenished with ink, a bucket
Which is being filled with asphalt;—making signs
From a ship, an arm equipped with a red signal, for a match
That is hard to extinguish;—for those which before one replaces it
Are visible on a cork, the words engraved on a log
From a sawn-up tree;—when, without ceremony, she leans with her
    elbow
Against a wall, the naked arm of an artist's model,
For an index finger as it taps;—when a mother daringly
Opens a cradle, its white curtains, for two leaves
In an uncut book one prises apart;—zigzagging without eyelets,

334   *fait trimer au tonneau*: Roussel is referring to the game *jeu de tonneau* (also known as *jeu de grenouille*), in which players set discs spinning with paddles; these discs are considerably smaller than the wheel of a water-mill.

336   *un porte-riflards plein*: The umbrella holder would have to be one that held its umbrellas horizontally one on top of the other to make it resemble the lines on music paper.

340   *jeu de grâces*: A game invented in the first quarter of the 19th century in which two sticks, each about 16 inches long, are used to propel a wicker ring into the air. In Roussel's comparison, the sticks are analogous to the fingers, and the ring to the mouth, of the whistler.

Instruction for illustration 28: The original Lemerre edition of *Nouvelles Impressions d'Afrique* had its pages uncut, and all its versos left blank; therefore, to see each of Zo's illustrations, readers would have had to prise apart two leaves, just as the reader in this one is doing.

A man seated at a table on which rests
an upright book, two of whose uncut
leaves he is prising apart in order to read
a passage. (lines 354–55)

Un pliant mètre jaune en passe de s'étendre,
Pour un lacet d'été mis;—quand pour plus l'entendre
Du va-et-vient l'enfant use, un cerceau sonneur,
Pour un cœur de montre;—en plein escalier d'honneur,
Une barre à tapis, pour la charnière en cuivre   360
D'un coffret se vidant;—pour le signe apte à suivre
Plaît-il, ce qu'un carlin noir, en marchant devant,
Montre à son maître;—pour ce qu'en y prélevant
Le dedans la cuiller ôte à l'œuf à la coque,
La calotte du pape;—un beau toit de bicoque   365
Neigeux, pour un bouquin docte étalé dos haut,
Frais vêtu d'écolier papier;—quand, comme il faut,
Fait un cheval au vert, le produit, pour des boules
De cochonnet en plein billard;—pour ce qu'aux poules
Râfle au passage l'œuf, les éclaboussements   370
D'un mollet à bas blanc;—d'angoissants ossements
Dans un bassin vidé, pour la part qu'a l'assiette
D'un suceur d'abatis;—pour deux dents qu'une miette
Disjoint, les deux doigts blancs d'un valet qui, gants mis,
Pouce oisif, ramasse un croûton;—lorsqu'en amis   375
Flânent deux noirs, leurs bras crochus, pour deux stupides
Hameçons emmêlés;—pour l'aiguille aux rapides
Parcours qu'enchanté d'elle un tailleur meut du pied,

A fold-up yellow meter-long ruler in the process of being extended,
For a shoelace worn in summer;—when, to hear it more often,
A child twirls a hoop with bells on,
For the wheel at the heart of a watch;—in the middle of the principal
    staircase,
A carpet bar, for the brass hinge
Of a small chest as it's emptied;—for the punctuation mark that
    normally follows
Plaît-il, that which a black pug dog, walking in front,
Shows to its owner;—for that which, setting it apart
From the rest inside, a spoon removes from a soft-boiled egg,
The Pope's skullcap;—the beautiful roof of a snowbound
Shack, for an erudite book laid down spine upwards,
That has been freshly covered in foolscap paper;—when, as it must,
A horse goes in a field, the result, for jacks used
In boules on a billiard table;—for that which, when hens lay,
The egg picks up in the course of its passage, splatterings
On a calf clad in a white stocking;—distressing remains
In an emptied reservoir, for the portion on the plate
Of a sucker of giblets;—for two teeth that a crumb
Separates, the two white-gloved fingers of a valet, who,
Without using his thumb, picks up a crust of bread;—when as friends
Two black men stroll, their arms that are hooked together, for two
    stupid
Entangled fishhooks;—for a rapidly progressing
Needle that a delighted tailor operates by foot,

361–62   *le signe apte à suivre / Plaît-il*: i.e., a question mark.

A snow-covered cottage whose roof has
the shape of a book laid face down, its
spine in the air. No people.
(lines 365–66)

Un marteau-pilon;—-lorsqu'un jour à frac s'assied
Un soigneux, ses pans qu'il ouvre, pour une paire   380
De faux favoris au repos;—pour un repaire
De dogue, adossé contre une clôture en fer,
Une guérite à grille;—un tison plein d'enfer
Dans une pince à feu, pour le rubis qu'exhibe
Celle d'un lapidaire;—un rond-de-cuir de scribe,   385
Pour celui qu'a pour nimbe un garçon pâtissier;
—Pour la poche à l'envers qui lorsque entre l'huissier
Sort d'un pantalon lâche, un plat sac à pitance
Pour museau de cheval;—pour deux dés en partance
Dans leur cornet, deux blancs cubes pris, de concert   390
Sucrant un gobelet vide;—géant qui sert
D'enseigne, pour celui qu'on fixe aux maisons dignes,
Un impur numéro;—pour celui dont les lignes
Fraîches à leurs secrets initient le buvard,
Un cylindre à parc;—pour un petit doigt bavard   395
Visant une enquêteuse oreille, un index raide
Qu'une narine attire à soi;—sobre offreur d'aide,
Un guide-âne, pour un échantillon rayé
De chemisier;—quand, preste, un crédule effrayé
Fait les cornes, sa main, pour la tête attentive   400
D'un limaçon rôdeur; pour la même inventive

A steam-hammer;—when, on a day that requires a morning-coat,
A careful man sits down, the opened tails of his jacket, for a pair
Of false whiskers lying idle;—for the kennel
Of a watchdog that backs onto a fence of railings,
A sentry box in front of an iron gate;—a glowing firebrand
In a pair of fire-tongs, for the ruby exhibited
In a jewel-expert's tweezers;—the round leather cushion of a copyist,
For that which a young pastry cook has for a halo;
—For the pocket turned inside out which, when the bailiff enters,
Emerges from a pair of loosely fitting trousers, a flat nosebag
For the muzzle of a horse;—for two dice as they leave
The dice-shaker, two white sugar cubes which together
Sweeten an empty goblet;—with its gigantic numerals
Serving as a sign, for that which is affixed to respectable houses,
The door number of a brothel;—for the cylinder that initiates
The blotter to the secrets of freshly written lines,
A heavy roller in a park;—for a talkative little finger
Aiming at an inquisitive ear, a stiff index finger
That a nostril attracts to itself;—sober provider of help,
The sheet of black ruled lines supplied with a writing pad, for a striped
    sample
From a shirtmaker;—when a credulous person receives a fright,
And quickly makes a pair of horns, his hand, for the careful head
Of a prowling snail; for the same inventive hand,

393   *Un impur numéro*: Possibly a reference to Le One-two-two, a brothel at 122 rue de Provence.

400–402   *Fait les cornes . . . asinal bonnet*: For illustrations of the way fingers making horns to ward off bad luck resemble the horns of a snail and the ears of a donkey cap, see Jean Ferry, *UE*, p.105.

A man seen in profile, seated at a desk (left profile) holding in his hand a page of black ruled lines that he is about to slip under a sheet of paper. (lines 397–98)

Main en blanc gant de luxe, un asinal bonnet;
—Quand s'est de l'oculiste ouvert le cabinet,
La pancarte au mur mise, en rang de lettres riche,
Pour un feuillet d'ABC;—pour un fou qui triche,   405
Quand de son glissement de tour elle fait choix,
La reine;—au sein d'un char funéraire, une croix
En violettes, pour une croix en poussière
D'améthystes à noir écrin;—une brassière
De wagon, pour le bout culotté d'un vieux stick;   410
—Pour les boulettes dont, à table, un gris loustic
Bombarde un bec d'ami, les sphères choquant, lourdes,
Un passe-boule;—un mur à béquilles, à Lourdes,
Pour la page à l'envers d'un zélé tout petit
A grands A;—le croûton par manque d'appétit   415
Laissé, quand la serviette y touche, non pliée,
Pour un doigt de gant à cordon blanc;—oubliée,
Une alliance en plein coin clair de lavabo,
Pour l'O d'or d'un pli chic;—cherchant l'absent bobo,
Pour un rouleau d'anglais taffetas, une pièce   420
D'enroulé satin rose;—un ballon, pour l'espèce
De capsule à filet qu'on fait vaporiser;
—Quand d'un bas on l'expulse, un œuf à repriser,
Pour ce qui d'une chèvre, avec retard, clôture

If it were wearing a white glove, a donkey cap;
—When the optician's consulting room is open,
The chart on the wall full of rows of letters,
For a child's ABC chart;—for a bishop that's cheating,
The queen when she moves
Sideways like a rook; —at the heart of a hearse, a cross
Made of violets, for a cross made with tiny
Amethysts in a black jewel case;—a hanging strap
In a railway carriage, for the seasoned end of an old riding-switch;
—For the meatballs with which, at table, a drunken joker
Pelts the mouth of a friend, heavy basketballs striking
A basketball hoop;—a wall with crutches leaned against it in Lourdes,
For an upside-down page of a zealous little child
Full of capital A's;—the end of a loaf left for lack of appetite
When an unfolded napkin touches it,
For the finger of a glove with a white ribbon trim;—a forgotten
Wedding ring on a bright corner of a basin,
For the golden O of a chic envelope;—for a roll of sticking plaster
That will make the hurt go away, a piece
Of rolled-up pink satin;—a balloon, for the type
Of net-covered capsule used in spray dispensers;
—When it's expelled from a stocking, a darning egg,
For that with which a goat eventually terminates

419   *bobo*: A nursery word for hurt or sore (like American "boo-boo").

A woman sitting in the corner of
a train carriage with her arm in a
hanging strap. (lines 409–10)

L'allègement;—pour un reste à mésaventure 425
De muette mitaine, une flûte de Pan;
—Pour l'oignon d'or qui fuit, taquinant son tympan,
D'un soupeur ivre à plat le gilet blanc, l'aphone
Bassinoire qu'on sort d'un lit;—dès qu'il plafonne,
Un échappé ballon d'enfant dans un ciel beau, 430
Pour un rouge pâté d'huissier;—un noir tableau
Qu'approprie un torchon, pour le front haut d'un nègre
Qui, s'épongeant, poisse un mouchoir; pour une allègre
Mine de plomb, son doigt humide ornant d'un nom
Un embué carreau; le même à dire « non » 435
Servant, horizontal, pour une pointe sombre
De boussole bougée;—attiédi donneur d'ombre,
Quand sévit l'astre, pour un couvre-nuque, un mur
De tente à toit plat;—pour un blanc cheveu de mûr
Blond, la sèche égayant un fouillis de havanes; 440
—Pour deux anneaux serrant mal des doigts diaphanes
D'amaigri, ceux au cirque où deux bras ont plongé;
—La feuille en plant où gît le compas en congé
D'un géomètre absent, pour une montre morte
Carrée;—à s'étonner prêt si l'étape est forte, 445
Pour un campylomètre utilisé, l'avant
D'une brouette au pas;—quand, d'un cheval savant,

The alleviation of its bowels;—for what remains after a speechless
    mitten
Has had an accident, a set of panpipes;
—For the gold watch that, teasing his eardrum, escapes
From the white waistcoat of a completely drunken diner, the voiceless
Warming pan that someone takes from a bed;—while it ascends,
A child's escaped balloon in a beautiful sky,
For the red blob of ink of a process-server;—a blackboard
That an eraser is rendering fit for duty, for the high forehead of a black
    man
Which, as he mops himself, moistens a handkerchief;—for a lively
Charcoal pencil, his wet finger adorning with a name
A misted windowpane; the same finger indicating "No,"
In a horizontal position, for the black needle
Of a shaken compass;—warmed giver of shade,
When the dog-star rages, for the sun-curtain of a cap, the wall
Of a tent with a flat roof;—for the white hair of a mature
Blond, the cigarette enlivening a miscellany of Havana cigars;
—For two rings that are much too big for the diaphanous fingers
Of someone emaciated, those at the circus into which two arms are
    plunged;
—The dog-eared sheet on which lies a pair of idle compasses
That belong to an absent geometrician, for a stopped, square
Watch;—for a map-measuring wheel used by someone
Ready to be amazed at the length of the journey, the front
Of a wheelbarrow;—when the rump of a performing horse

426   *mitaine*: For the visual comparison to work the mitten must really be a glove, and have lost in its "*mésaventure*" the top of each of its fingers.

A man using a map-measurer
on a map.(lines 445–46)

La croupe a décrit son rond, pour une torsade,
Ses jambes de devant fixes;—par temps maussade,
Quand la prolonge un V, l'aiguille à bons conseils,   450
Pour le bout d'un cheveu fourchu;—pour deux orteils
Vus par un trou de bas, ce qu'encadre un malade
Fond de culotte;—pour de la lourde salade
Parmentière, des *blancs* qu'en tas sur un damier
Met un bavard aux doigts distraits;—pour le premier   455
Papier soyeux tombé d'une carte cornée,
Un gris dallage en verre uni;—pour ce qu'ornée
De clous une semelle a dans la crotte empreint,
Un solitaire sans billes;—lorsqu'il n'étreint
Rien, un saint brassard blanc, en montre, pour un brave   460
Nœud tout fait du soir;—noire, une moustache à grave
Manque de nerf, si la mouche meuble son arc,
Pour un point d'orgue;—quand brille à la pluie un parc,
L'intact fond d'un brisé pot de terre, pour une
Jaune paillette à trou;—lorsqu'ils choient à la brune,   465
Pour des haricots verts sautant d'un plat, d'étroits
Feuillets de jalousie; et tard, dans les endroits
Commerçants, d'entassés plis jaunes, pour des pommes
Qu'un fricoteur souffla mal;—pour ces gais bonshommes
En papier qu'un plafond balance au bout d'un fil,   470

Has twisted around in a circling maneuver, for a plaited fringe,
Its fixed front legs;—in cheerless weather,
The barometer's needle that is extended because it's pointing at V,
For the end of a split hair;—for two toes
Seen through a hole in a stocking, that which is framed by a distressed
Trouser seat;—for a heavy Parmentier salad,
The white chips that are formed into a pile on the checkerboard
By a chatty fellow with distracted fingers;—for the first
Sheet of silky tissue paper that falls from a dog-eared map,
A grey glass paving slab;—for that which the sole
Of a hobnailed boot has imprinted in droppings,
A solitaire board without pegs;—when it's not wrapped around
Anything, a wholly white armband, on show, for a gallant
Ready-made evening bow-tie;—a black, drooping
Moustache, if in the middle of its arc there is a tuft on the lower lip,
For the musical notation for a pause;—when a park glistens in the
    rain,
The intact base of a broken flowerpot, for a yellow
Spangle with a hole in the middle;—the narrow slats of a Venetian
    blind
When they are lowered at dusk, for green beans
Falling from a plate; and later, in commercial
Districts, piles of yellow envelopes, for potatoes
With which a cook has made a bad soufflé;—for the funny gay paper
    figures
That swing from a ceiling at the end of a thread,

450   *un V*: The V on the barometer the needle is pointing to is for Variable.

453–54   *la lourde salade / Parmentière*: Parmentier salad includes sliced potatoes; these both make it heavy, and resemble a pile of white pieces in checkers.

A woman lowering the Venetian blind of a window. The blind is already half closed, the slats almost horizontal. (lines 465–67)

Les pendus après la neige;—fruit d'un civil
Baiser, l'aqueux rond d'un gant blanc, pour une marque
D'égoutté chalumeau;—pour celle qu'un monarque
A pour hochet, la main faite en marbre d'après
La dextre d'une belle;—entiché du progrès,   475
Un Peau-Rouge en complet, pour un môme à rougeole;
—Vu ses rayures, pour une prise rigole
A glissade de choix, un usagé chemin
A lancer les vaisseaux;—pour un bec sans carmin
D'anémique au lit qui fume, un poing à bougie;   480
—Quand queute un effronté, sa bille non rougie,
Pour une perle ronde à tige d'or pâli
Qu'on sort d'un ruban vert;—l'appendice poli
D'un chien gris, pour l'antenne à bruit d'un métronome;
—Pour l'interne rectangle où le tailleur nous nomme,   485
La suscription mise, une enveloppe aux durs
Flancs de toile;—rageuse injuste à coups futurs,
La mailloche, au concert, pour un bout débonnaire
D'appui-main;—pour la fente à rond d'un ordinaire
Protège-mine, un vide asile à boutons lourds;   490
—Pour deux sabots à chocs réchauffants d'orteils gourds,
Deux sauteurs bateaux à l'ancre en temps d'équinoxe
Se heurtant face à face;—un jour sans match de boxe,

Those who have been hanged after it has snowed;—the result of a civil
Kiss, a wet ring on a white glove, for a mark
Made by a used drinking straw;—for that which a monarch
Has for a bauble, the hand made in marble modelled
On the right hand of a beautiful woman;—infatuated with progress,
A Red Indian in a suit, for a kid with measles;
—In light of their grooves, for a frozen channel
To be slid down however one wants, a ramp used
To launch ships;—for the very pale mouth
Of an anemic who is smoking in bed, a fist holding a candle;
—When a rakish type cues off, the non-red ball that he strikes,
For a round pearl on a stem of pale gold
That's being taken out of a green ribbon;—the polite appendage
Of a grey dog, for the noisy antenna of a metronome;
—For the rectangle sewn into clothes on which a tailor names us,
A parcel, with the address written on it, wrapped
In stiff cloth;—choleric and unfair when, in the future, it will deal out
    blows,
The bass drumstick at a concert, for the good-natured end
Of a painter's maulstick;—for the round opening of an ordinary
Screw-pencil, a large empty button-stick;
—For two clogs being knocked together to warm frozen toes,
Two boats pitching at anchor in equinoctial weather
And colliding bow to bow;—on a day on which there is no boxing
    match,

473–74   *pour celle qu'un monarque / A pour hochet*: A reference to the *main de justice*, a scepter topped by an ivory hand which became part of the French Crown Jewels in the 13th century.

483   *l'appendice poli*: i.e., the dog's wagging tail.

485   *l'interne rectangle*: As well as this internal rectangle with his address on it, Roussel also had sewn into the lining of all of his suits and overcoats a small square of material on which he kept a tally of its use: after an item had been worn fifteen times it was passed to his valet.

490   *vide asile à boutons lourds*: A gigantic button-stick and various large pencils feature in the performance of the chemist Bex in chapter 3 of *Impressions d'Afrique*. It is possible that he hoped initiates into his work would read this as another self-reference.

493   *un jour sans match de boxe*: It is because a boxing glove and a leather football are roughly the same size that Roussel specifies that there is no boxing match on this particular day.

Two men in clogs, in snowy weather,
knocking their soles together to warm
up their feet. (line 491)

Un ballon de cuir qui part, pour un ganté poing
Offensif;—un talon correct dont, récent point   495
De mire, un chanceux dix de pique est la retourne,
Pour un double-cinq;—pour le poil gris qui séjourne
Dans l'épileuse pince exploratrice, un fil
De fer dont s'est rendu maître un étau viril;
—Pour une humble chapelle où la tête se cogne,   500
La cathédrale monstre assise en plein Cologne;
—Le brutal iceberg, du pôle nord natif,
Pour l'étroit bloc de glace asservi, portatif,
Qu'en morceaux pour le verre, à l'office, on brésille;
—Chez un pêcheur, pour un pou dans une résille,   505
Une oisive araignée explorant un chalut;)))),
Cherche un coup d'encensoir à joindre à son salut:
Pour qu'à lui vienne la fortune, dont la roue
((((Témoin:—le gros banquier qu'on file et qu'on écroue;
—Le grinche en paix, la nuit, jouant du rossignol;   510
—Le Commissaire alors que le rosse Guignol;
—Samson faible allant la dextre en avant;—Turenne
Quand, de la bonne sorte, à Salzbach il étrenne;
—L'absinthe à l'hypocondre ouvrant le paradis;
—L'Enfant prodigue au nid rentrant sans un radis;   515
—L'héritier plein de plans qui, près du catafalque,

A leather ball in flight, for a gloved, attacking
Fist;—a pack of cards onto which, to general recent
Amazement, a lucky ten of spades has just been turned over,
For a double five in dominoes;—for the grey hair held
By an exploring pair of tweezers, a steel wire
In the grip of a virile vice;
—For a humble chapel in which one bangs one's head,
The monstrously large cathedral in the middle of Cologne;
—The brutal iceberg, a native of the North Pole,
For the narrow easily carried block of ice which is made to serve us,
Broken into small pieces suitable for drinks in the pantry;
—At a fisherman's, for a louse in a hairnet,
A lazy spider exploring a dragnet;)))),
Tries to come up with a bit of fulsome flattery to add to his welcome:
In order that he should be blessed by good fortune, whose wheel
((((As witness:—the big banker who is shadowed and jailed;
—The reformed thief at peace, at night, playing with his skeleton keys;
—The Commissioner when Punch thrashes him;
—Enfeebled Samson walking with his right hand out in front;—
    Turenne
When he received a setback to his good fortune at Salzbach;
—Absinthe opening paradise to a hypochondriac;
—The prodigal son returning to the nest without a sou;
—The heir who's full of plans, and by the catafalque

507 *Cherche un coup d'encensoir*: This returns us to line 37 and the patron whose awareness of human foibles, in particular human vanity, leads him to flatter his customers when they arrive.

508 *dont la roue*: After a mere 26 examples of turns of the wheel of fortune, we return to this syntactic unit at line 541.

509 (((((*Témoin*: The occasion, along with the *témoin* in line 63 of Canto III, of the *Contre-Erratum* that Roussel had inserted at the end of the poem, in which he instructs the reader that "*c'est volontairement que le mot* témoin *a été mis au singulier*" ("the word *witness* has been deliberately put in the singular"). We are not to suppose an error; instead we should mentally insert a single *témoin* before each of the examples that follow.

512 *Turenne*: A reference to Henri de la Tour d'Auvergne, Vicomte de Turenne, Marshall of France. A brilliant strategist, Turenne (as he was generally known) was killed in the course of Louis XIV's Dutch War at the battle of Salzbach on July 27, 1675.

A drinker who seems to be
approaching a state of ecstasy.
No other people. (line 514)

Tout bas additionne, arrondit et défalque;
—L'amiral commençant de ronfler sans effroi
Puis de Germain d'Auxerre entendant le beffroi;
—Cinna conspirateur, devenant sur son siège   520
L'ami d'Auguste après avoir flairé le piège;
—Le soulier visité par le petit Jésus;
—L'odalisque à qui fut jeté le tire-jus;
—Le téméraire qui passe une pièce fausse;
—Daniel sympathique aux lions dans la fosse;   525
—L'œuf effacé qu'illustre à jamais rend Colomb
En lui persuadant de se tenir d'aplomb;
—Lourdes en petit fou changeant un grand malade;
—Le faux prince tâtant du panier à salade;
—Quand, voyant dans son mur Gretchen, il porte un toast   530
Puis s'ôte en buvant dix lustres, le docteur Faust;
—Le mal qui foudroie en plein bonheur les toupies;
—L'inventeur riche à sec mis par ses utopies;
—Le lac de cire obscur quand, bravant la cuisson,
Un résolu cachet lui flanque un écusson;   535
—Le pion à destin qu'un changement de case
Fait dame;—Prométhée aux fers sur le Caucase;
—Le chat dorloté puis cuit de la mèr' Michel;
—L'enfant cossu volé par un romanichel;

Under his breath adds up, rounds up, and deducts;
—The Admiral beginning to snore peacefully,
Then hearing the warning bell of St. Germain l'Auxerrois;
—Cinna the conspirator, becoming there and then
The friend of Augustus, having got wind of a trap;
—The shoe visited by the little Jesus;
—The harem-girl at whom a handkerchief was thrown;
—The reckless one who pays with a false coin;
—Daniel liked by the lions in the den;
—The long lost egg that made Columbus forever famous
By persuading him to keep his nerve;
—Lourdes changing a great invalid into a little fool;
—The false prince trying out a prison van;
—When, seeing Gretchen in the wall, he proposes a toast,
Then becomes fifty years younger, Doctor Faustus;
—The illness that strikes down old frumps in the midst of their
    happiness;
—The rich inventor bankrupted by his utopias;
—The humble lake of wax, when, braving the burning pain,
A resolute seal thrusts a shield into him;
—The pawn destined for high things that a change of square
Makes into a queen;—Prometheus in chains in the Caucasus;
—The cat that was petted, then cooked, of mèr' Michel;
—The wealthy child stolen by a gypsy;

518–19   *L'amiral . . . Germain d'Auxerre*: A reference to Lord Gaspard de Coligny (1519–1572). Coligny was a fierce Huguenot, and held the office of Admiral of France. His murder in Paris sparked the St. Bartholomew's Day Massacres of August 1572. In some accounts, the signal for the attack was given by ringing bells for matins at the church of Saint-Germain l'Auxerrois, near the Louvre. The church is named in honour of St. Germain, Bishop of Auxerre (c. 380–448).

520   *Cinna*: A reference to Pierre Corneille's *Cinna* (1639). Cinna and Maxine scheme to kill the Emperor Augustus, but fall out with each other on discovering that they are both in love with the same woman, Émilie. After much plotting and counter-plotting, all is discovered to Augustus; the Emperor decides, however, to forgive those involved in the conspiracy, and Cinna is transformed "*sur son siège*" from Augustus's enemy into his friend.

522   *Le soulier visité par le petit Jésus*: A reference to a French Catholic Christmas tradition, similar to the Christmas stocking, in which children leave a shoe by the Christmas tree on Christmas Eve, and overnight "*le petit Jésus*" fills it with presents.

523   *le tire-jus*: The handkerchief signals to the concubine that she has been selected for her master's bed.

526   *l'œuf effacé*: Columbus is supposed to have compared the difficulty of discovering America to the seemingly impossible task of making an egg stand up—which he accomplished by tapping it on the table and so flattening its end.

530–31   *Gretchen . . . Faust*: A reference to a scene in Act I of Gounod's *Faust* (1859). Mephistopheles appears to the despairing Faust in his study, where he conjures up an image of Gretchen at her spinning wheel that persuades Faust to exchange his services in hell for Mephistopheles's services on earth. Celebrating the pact with a toast, the ageing scholar is transformed into a handsome young nobleman.

532   *Le mal qui foudroie en plein bonheur les toupies*: Another possible self-reference. In chapter 5 of *Impressions d'Afrique* the ageing ballerina Olga Tcherwonenkoff is struck down by a sudden pain while performing *le Pas de la Nymphe*. The source of the incident is given in "Comment j'ai écrit. . ." as *toupie à coup de fouet* (*CJ*, p. 17).

538   *Le chat dorloté puis cuit de la mèr' Michel*: A reference to the children's song in which mèr' Michel laments the loss of her beloved cat, and is answered by pèr' Lustucru that it is not lost, but sold as a rabbit, i.e., to be cooked and eaten.

An elegantly dressed man
pressing a seal into a pool of wax
on a letter. (lines 534–35)

—Cendrillon finissant par devenir princesse;)))),   540
Mouvant ses ailerons, tourne sans paix ni cesse,
—Tel, devant son nombril, le chapeau d'un benêt,—
Tout hôte flatte, écoute—opine du bonnet
Même alors qu'on soutient:—que garder une somme
Jamais d'un savetier ne compromit le somme;   545
—Qu'un nain qui vous vient dans la glace à l'abdomen
Vous paraîtrait géant placé sous un dolmen;
—Qu'il faut, quand c'est servi, de force attabler l'homme
Qui d'un ver solitaire à sa charge est le home;
—Qu'amène est d'instinct la femme envers son mari   550
Plus que la vieille fille envers son canari;
—Qu'outre-Manche à certains essuyages intimes,
En aveugle accomplis, jamais ne sert le *Times*;
—Qu'un phtisique à Paris, plus vite qu'à Menton,
Rien que par le calme et l'air double son menton;   555
—Qu'en l'honneur de l'asperge, en mai, lorsqu'il urine,
Jamais gourmet repu n'enfle, œil clos, sa narine;
—Qu'ignare en son bocal, la rainette, selon
Son seul caprice, adopte ou lâche un échelon;
—Qu'une mouche accentue en y tirant sa coupe   560
L'attrait par le breuvage exercé dans la coupe;
—Qu'il en coûte au frileux de relever son col

—Cinderella who ends up becoming a princess;)))),
Moving its wings, turns without peace or rest,
—Just like the hat of a simpleton, as he turns it in front of his navel,—
Every host flatters, listens—nods his head
Even if it is being claimed:—that keeping a sum of money
Never disturbed the sleep of a cobbler;
—That a dwarf who comes up to your stomach in a mirror
Would seem to you a giant if placed under a dolmen;
—That it's necessary, when dinner is served, to force to the table a
    man
Who is home to a tapeworm that is dependent on him;
—That a wife is kind by instinct towards her husband
More than an old woman towards her canary;
—That on the other side of the Channel, for certain intimate wipings
Accomplished without looking, the *Times* is never used;
—That a consumptive in Paris, more quickly than in Menton,
Will, through calm and good air, double the size of his chin;
—That in honor of the asparagus, in May, when he urinates,
A sated gourmet never closes his eyes and flares his nostrils;
—That, ignorant in its goldfish bowl, the tree frog is prompted
Only by its own whims to make use of or abandon its ladder;
—That a fly accentuates, by drinking its fill there,
The attraction exerted by a beverage in a cup;
—That it's an effort for those sensitive to the cold to raise their collars

541   *Mouvant ses ailerons*: Lines 541–44 pick up from line 508: In order that he should be blessed by Fortune, whose winged wheel turns without rest, every host flatters, listens, nods his head.

544   *qu'on soutient:—* : Roussel proceeds to offer 29 examples (in lines 544–601) of absurd claims that a host, in his eagerness to flatter, would agree were true.

545   *un savetier:* A reference to La Fontaine's "*Le Savetier et le Financier*" ("The Cobbler and the Financier"), in which a light-hearted cobbler suffers terrible insomnia after being given a bag of money by his financier neighbor.

554   *Menton*: Town on the French Riviera. During his trip around the world of 1920–21, Roussel visited a town called Menton in Australia. In a postcard he sent from Melbourne to Charlotte Dufrène, he noted: "Near here there are two bathing resorts which are called Brighton and Menton. It's well worth the trouble of coming so far to make excursions to Brighton and Menton, which is what I've done" (*RC*, 210–11).

558   *la rainette*: Tree frogs are reputed to be able to predict the weather. Its use or non-use of its ladder is prompted, therefore, not by whim, but by a forthcoming change in meteorological conditions.

A man of average height next to a dwarf
who comes up to his stomach. The
pair are seen from the back in front of
a large mirror that reflects them; they
seem to want to compare their heights.
(lines 546–47)

Quand le mercure gèle et fait place à l'alcool;
—Que rien n'est, du pays, semblable à la bottine,
Où l'abeille en tout temps, d'après Mignon, butine;   565
—Qu'un poltron recevrait sans secousse un cartel
Pourvu que de nul autre il ne vînt que de Tell;
—Que le feu fît aux rois plus bas courber l'échine
Qu'en stratège émérite alluma Rostopchine;
—Qu'un libéré bouchon, mieux qu'un bas, lorsq'il part,   570
Traverserait un haut plafond de part en part;
—Que, des astres, plus ronde est la lune et plus crue
Sa clarté, plus la somme, autour d'elle, est accrue;
—Qu'en l'art nul n'égala Napoléon Iᵉʳ
D'éviter de manger son pain blanc le premier;   575
—Qu'à nu mis les travers de la femme savante
Jamais n'ont de Molière égayé la servante;
—Qu'unanime un refus s'oppose à qui, poli,
Demande aux gens licence avant d'ouvrir un pli;
—Que si le spécimen noir rare est chez la perle   580
Plus que le blanc, de même il en va chez le merle;
—Que lorsqu'on l'a servi bien le joueur de *Nain
Jaune* adore finir sans avoir eu la main;
—Que c'est lors d'un de ses étés qu'ému d'une aune
De son manteau l'humain saint Martin fit l'aumône;   585

When mercury freezes and gives way to an alcohol-filled thermometer;
—That in no way does it resemble a boot, that country
Where the bee, according to Mignon, gathers pollen from flowers all
    year long;
—That a coward will receive without quaking a challenge to a duel
As long as it comes from none other than William Tell;
—That it made kings grovel and fawn still further, the fire
That in a celebrated stratagem Rostopchin started in Moscow;
—That a liberated cork, when it leaves the bottle, will more easily
Pierce the ceiling of a high room than that of a low one;
—That the fuller and brighter the moon is,
The greater the number of stars gathered around her;
—That Napoleon wasn't pre-eminent in the art
Of avoiding eating his white bread first;
—That seeing the failings of a female intellectual laid bare
Never amused the maid in a Molière play;
—That a unanimous refusal will be the response to someone
Who politely asks permission to open a letter in public;
—That if a black pearl is rarer than
A white one, the same goes for blackbirds;
—That when he has been dealt a hand at *Nain*
Jaune, a player likes finishing the game without having had the lead;
—That it was in the midst of one of his own summers that, moved,
St Martin gave as alms a section of his own coat;

563   *l'alcool*: Ethanol-filled thermometers are used in preference to mercury ones to measure very low temperatures.

565   *Mignon*: Mignon is a character in the popular comic opera *Mignon* (1866) by Ambroise Thomas. The heroine Mignon sings, referring to Italy, that country "*semblable à la bottine*":

> *Connais-tu le pays où fleurit l'oranger?*
> *Le pays des fruits d'or et des roses merveilles,*
> *Où la brise est plus douce et l'oiseau plus léger,*
> *Où dans toute saison butinent les abeilles . . .*

> Do you know the land where the orange tree blossoms?
> The country of golden fruits and marvelous roses,
> Where the breeze is softer and birds lighter,
> Where in every season bees gather pollen . . .

569   *Rostopchine*: Fyodor Rostopchin (1763–1826) was governor of Moscow during Napoleon's invasion of Russia. The burning of Moscow, which he may well have instigated, is presented here by Roussel as crucial in the defeat of the French forces, and therefore as having played a part in restoring the monarchies of Europe.

575   *D'éviter de manger son pain blanc*: A reference to the story that in his childhood Napoleon would keep his white bread and exchange it with a soldier for a piece of coarse brown bread; he did this in order to grow accustomed to military fare.

582–83   *Nain / Jaune*: *le jeu du Nain Jaune* (the game of the Yellow Dwarf) is a traditional French card game. To win you need to have the lead as often as possible.

585   *saint Martin*: It was in the middle of winter that Saint Martin gave half his coat to a beggar. Cf. Canto I, lines 80–81.

William Tell aiming at the apple
placed on his son's head. No
other people. (line 567)

—Qu'en amour nul ne sut faire à l'égal d'Onan
Passer avant tout la loi du *donnant donnant*;
—Qu'est l'effet détruit moins bien que par un bécarre
D'une altération par la prochaine barre;
—Qu'à sa voisine à sec, jadis, par la fourmi,   590
Tout fut, quand vint la bise, obligeamment fourni;
—Qu'Attila, mieux campé que son aîné Rodrigue,
D'alexandrins fameux est plus que lui prodigue;
—Qu'un trait courbe, à l'encontre allant d'un bruit qui court,
Pour marier deux points plus qu'une droite est court;   595
—Qu'un houleux débat lorsqu'on sonne s'envenime;
—Que l'arme la plus noble est la lettre anonyme
Pour battre ses rivaux dans la course aux honneurs[1]

1. Que de prospérités, que de fermes bonheurs
   Pour qui n'est point aveugle ont une source infâme!
   Le prix de piano dépend plus pour la femme
   Du nombre de galants qu'elle a dans le jury
   Que de son déchiffrage et du talent mûri   5
   Qu'elle déploie ou non en jouant sa sonate;
   Maint X . . .-les-Bains doit moins à son bicarbonate
   Qu'aux joueurs qui, la nuit, hantent son casino.

—That in the matter of love none equalled Onan
In privileging above all the ideal of giving;
—That, in music, the effect of an alteration is destroyed less well
By a natural sign than by the next bar;
—That, long ago, to its starving neighbor, the ant
Obligingly provided all he could when the icy blasts of winter came;
—That the character Atilla was better performed than his predecessor
    Rodrigue,
And also delivers more famous alexandrine couplets;
—That a curved line, when one is proceeding towards a noise in the
    distance,
Is shorter than a straight line in going from one point to another;
—That a rowdy debate grows more acrimonious when the bell is rung;
—That the anonymous letter is the most noble weapon
With which to defeat one's rivals in the race for honors[1]

1. How much prosperity, how much steady happiness,
   As anyone who is not blind can see, has an infamous source!
   The piano prize depends more for a woman contestant
   On how many admirers she has on the jury
   Than on her sight-reading and the developed talent
   That she displays, or doesn't, when performing her sonata;
   Many X . . . -les-Bains owe less to their bicarbonate waters
   Than to the gamblers who frequent the town's casino at night.

586   *Onan*: The son of Judah, who, when instructed to have sex with Tamar, the widow of his brother Er, "spilled [his seed] on the ground" rather than impregnate her (Genesis 38:9).

590   *le fourmi*: A reference to La Fontaine's fable of "*La Cigale et la fourmi*" ("The Cricket and the Ant"): having spent all summer playing, the cricket asks the industrious ant for some food when winter comes. The ant refuses.

592   *Attila . . . Rodrigue*: Rodrigue is the hero of Corneille's immensely successful *Le Cid* (1636), and hence the *aîné*, the older brother or predecessor of the central protagonist of the late *Attila*, a play that was given only a short run when first performed in 1667, and has not proved popular with critics or public since.

A rowdy assembly. On a dais the president is ringing his bell. (line 596)

—Lettre que, révolté, le digne Calino
Sans la décacheter jetait dans la corbeille— 600
Ou que la loi salique existe chez l'abeille;)))
Deux couteaux cliquetants qu'affûte un découpeur;)),
Veste au dos, feutre au front,—objet si peu trompeur,—
Un brevet pour l'oiseau de foncière bêtise;),
Surtout gris, chapeau noir (dont l'aspect synthétise 605
Ces temps où l'on voyait des rois partis de rien
Et qu'inlassablement fouille l'historien;),
Mis par lui jusqu'au bout sur son rocher accore,
Ne magnifiaient pas sa silhouette encore,
Fait que, méditatif, on oublie un moment 610
L'Égypte, son soleil, ses soirs, son firmament.

—It was an anonymous letter that, disgusted, the noble Calino
Threw into the wastepaper basket without opening it—
Or that the Salic Law is observed by bees;)))
Two clinking knives that a carver sharpens;)),
A jacket on its back, a felt hat on its head,—a creation by no means
    convincing,—
A proof of the basic stupidity of birds;),
Grey greatcoat, black hat (the sight of which encapsulates
That period which witnessed the emergence of kings from nowhere,
And into which the historian tirelessly delves;),
Worn by him to the end on his sheer-cliffed rock,
Did not yet glorify his silhouette,
Makes one meditative, and forget for a moment
Egypt, its sun, its evenings, and its skies.

599   *Calino*: A stock name for a simpleton, deriving from the character Calinot of *Une Voiture de masques* (1856) by the Goncourt brothers. If Roussel's "*digne Calino*" threw the letter he received into the wastepaper basket without opening it, how did he know it was anonymous?

601   *la loi salique*: A law excluding women from succession to the throne.

602   *Deux couteaux*: The last of the examples of things that form a cross, and picking up from line 31.

603   *Veste au dos, feutre au front*: Turn back to the canto's first illustration, no. 12, to see the scarecrow's unconvincing trappings, and to line 10, for the first part of this clause.

608   *son rocher accore*: i.e., Saint Helena, to which Napoleon was exiled after his defeat at Waterloo.

A waiter with a pair of crossed knives that he is using to carve a roast chicken. No other people. (lines 30–31 and 602)

III

La Colonne qui, léchée jusqu'à ce que la langue saigne, guérit la jaunisse

MOSQUÉE ABOU'L-MA'ATÊH—ENVIRONS DE DAMIETTE

Traitement héroïque! user avec la langue,
Sans en rien rengainer qu'elle ne soit exsangue,
Après mille autres fous, les flancs de ce pilier!
Mais vers quoi ne courir, à quoi ne se plier,
Fasciné par l'espoir, palpable ou chimérique   5
(Espoir! roi des leviers! tout oncle d'Amérique
((Ce pays jeune encore, inépuisé, béni,
—Si tard, de nos atlas, vierge il resta banni,—
Où l'on rafle plus d'or, vingt fois, qu'en l'ancien monde,
Soit que—l'appétissant a besoin de l'immonde—   10
Par cent mille kilos on fabrique un engrais
Pour ces champs infinis, où, gaillards, le nez frais
(((Un jour, d'un chien souffrant fait un chien hydrophobe;

III

The column that, when licked until the tongue bleeds, cures jaundice

ABU EL-MAATI MOSQUE—OUTSKIRTS OF DAMIETTA

A treatment for heroes! to abrade with one's tongue
Without returning it to the mouth until it's drained of blood,
After a thousand other idiots, the sides of this pillar!
But what will a person not pursue, to what not submit,
When bewitched by the hope, whether real or fantastical
(Hope! king of levers! every wealthy *oncle d'Amérique*
((That country still young, unexhausted, blest—
—For, virgin territory, it was until only recently excluded from our
    atlases—
Where each amasses twenty times more gold than in the Old World,
Whether one—that which is appetizing depends on the filthy—
Manufactures by the hundredweight manure
For its endless fields, where, vigorous, with fresh, keen noses
(((Just one day can change a dog that's unwell into one that's
    hydrophobic;

MOSQUÉE ABOU'L-MA'ATÊH: The Abu El-Maati Mosque is in the cemetery district of El-Gabbana, northeast of Damietta. The column in question is in the southwest corner of the mosque.

5   *palpable ou chimérique*: Turn to the canto's final line (110) for continuation and completion of this opening clause.

6   *oncle d'Amérique*: A term for an uncle from whom one hopes to inherit money. To find out how he treats the nephews who nurture great expectations, turn to lines 106–9.

7   *ce pays jeune encore*: On a number of occasions Roussel plays off Europe against the Americas. In lines 147–48 of Canto I the Old and the New Worlds compete against each other for the eminent violinist who has himself photographed with his violin at his neck, and the late stories gathered under the title *Documents pour servir du canevas* (*Documents to Serve as an Outline*) were, we learn from the preliminary fragment "A la Havane" ("In Havana"), intended to illustrate the superiority of Europe to the Americas. His play of 1927, *La Poussière de soleils* (*The Dust of Suns*), is set in French Guyana. Roussel travelled across the United States in the course of his 1920–21 trip around the world, and seems to have been unimpressed by the democratic ideals of America. His psychiatrist Pierre Janet records him complaining: "On arrival in New York, I want to take a bath, and the idea of this gives me a certain pleasure. I learn that there are three thousand bathrooms in the hotel, and that three thousand travellers can take a bath at the same time; my pleasure disappears" (*De l'angoisse à l'extase*, vol. II, p. 148).

12   *le nez frais*: To follow this syntactic unit, turn to the second half of line 34, and then to line 52.

A joyful-looking man with
heaps of gold coins in front of
him, which he is in the process of
putting in orderly piles. (line 9)

S'assurer que toujours ce liquide que gobe
Même le mieux appris entre les nouveau-nés   15
Sort de l'ami de l'homme et lui vernit le nez
N'est pas, prenons-y garde, acte moins nécessaire
Que:—lorsque l'ennemi se fend d'un émissaire,
Sur les yeux de l'intrus appliquer un bandeau;
—Quand passe un roi, marquer autour de son landau   20
Chaque point cardinal par un mouchard cycliste;
—Quand, chef de conjurés, des noms on fait la liste,
Tout ce qu'on a d'esprit le mettre à la chiffrer;
—Pour que l'oiseau pillard hésite à s'empiffrer,
Meubler d'épouvantails les terres où l'on sème;   25
—Vieux ((((pendant notre hiver notre tignasse essaime,
Tels les rayons plantés dans le soleil vernal
S'en vont quand il se change en soleil hivernal;)))),
S'imposer de fuir l'air ou de porter calotte;
—Après avoir sombré de culotte en culotte,   30
Mettre en sûr viager l'argent sauvé du club;
—Engager le verrou quand c'est l'heure du tub;
—Avant de travailler sur une corde raide
S'armer d'un balancier;))), cent chiens prêtent leur aide
(((Besoin d'aide! ô besoin sublime, universel!   35
Combien mettraient des jours, sans aide, à voir le sel

To make sure always that this liquid, which is slurped down
By even the best brought up of newborn babies,
Both passes out of the friend of man and makes its nose glisten,
Is, take careful note, an act no less necessary
Than:—when the enemy sends forth an emissary,
To apply a bandage to the eyes of the intruder;
—When a king passes, to have covered each
Cardinal point around his landau by a police spy on a bicycle;
—When the chief conspirator makes a list of names
To use all possible ingenuity in devising a code for it;
—In order that pillaging birds hesitate to stuff themselves,
To install scarecrows on all the lands one cultivates;
—When old ((((during our winter our mop of hair departs,
Just as the rows of crops planted in the sun of spring
Disappear when it turns to a winter sun;)))),
To make oneself either avoid the open air or wear a skullcap;
—Having lost heavily over and over again,
To put into a secure life annuity the money saved from the gambling
    club;
—To bolt the door when it's time for a bath;
—Before setting out on a tightrope
To equip oneself with a balancing pole;))), a hundred dogs lend their
    aid
(((Need for aid! O need sublime and universal!
How many days, without help, would it take to grasp the wit

16   *Sort de l'ami de l'homme et lui vernit le nez*: Since one of the symptoms of rabies is fear of water, one must make certain that one's dog is getting its nose glistening wet from drinking in its water bowl, and that it consistently urinates.

18   *Que*: There follow eight examples of acts that are no less necessary than making sure one's dog is not hydrophobic (lines 18–34).

18   *se fend d'un émissaire*: Cf. Canto III, line 327, and Zo's illustration, no. 27.

34   *cent chiens prêtent leur aide*: This picks up the syntactic unit interrupted at line 12; it is returned to at line 52.

35   *(((Besoin d'aide!*: There follow seven examples that illustrate the importance of acts of helping (lines 36–51).

A man laboriously drawing up a list of names (if the names are legible, they must be in code). (lines 22–23)

Dont sont sursaturés un mot, une anecdote!
Pour que le perroquet distinctement radote
Faut-il pas qu'un de nous lui coupe le filet?
L'empereur, la main tiède au sortir du gilet, 40
Stimulait son génie en humant une prise;
Le superstitieux dont le miroir se brise
Dans sa détresse invite à conjurer le sort
Deux de ses doigts qui, mus comme par un ressort,
Prennent, en se tendant, l'allure de deux cornes; 45
L'argument—au pouvoir du geste il est des bornes—
Éclaire, d'un ballet, l'imbroglio naïf;
Grâce à l'ongle on peut voir les secrets d'un canif,
Sous un alinéa creuser un trait fragile;
Le jus du raisin pris, exploratrice agile, 50
La langue, de partout, chasse pépins et peaux;)))
A cent bergers de qui dépendent cent troupeaux;
Soit qu'on ouvre un hôtel dans l'air sain d'une cime
Chère aux débilités du monde richissime;
Soit que par stocks on vende à l'agioteur snob 55
(((Le rôle du snobisme ((((au vrai qu'était Jacob?[1]

---

1. Même est-on sûr que Dieu, quand il fit le snobisme
   (Si l'animal ne sait pas plus percer un isthme

With which a joke or anecdote is salted!
So that the parrot can spout its drivel clearly
Is it is not necessary for one of us to cut its frenum?
The Emperor, withdrawing his warm hand from his waistcoat,
Stimulates his genius by taking a pinch of snuff;
The superstitious person, if a mirror breaks,
In his distress attempts to ward off bad luck
With two of his fingers which, moved as if by a spring,
Assume, as he extends them, the appearance of two horns;
The plot synopsis—there are limits to the power of gestures—
Illuminates the naive imbroglio of a ballet;
Thanks to a fingernail one can see the secrets of a penknife,
Under the first line of a paragraph scratch a faint mark;
The juice of the grape squeezed out, that agile explorer
The tongue expels from all corners of the mouth the skin and seeds;)))
To a hundred shepherds on whom depend a hundred flocks;
Whether one opens a hotel in some healthy high-altitude spot
Much favored by wealthy invalids;
Whether one sells in heaps to the speculator who's a snob
((((The role played by snobbery ((((in essence, what was Jacob?[1]

---

1. Can one even be sure that God, when he made snobbery
    (If animals no more know how to build a canal across an isthmus

53   *Soit qu'on*: This returns to the theme of how people get rich in America, launched with the manure manufacturer of line 11. The canto presents five further examples, all introduced by *soit que*, at lines 53, 55, 61 (which has two, the founder of a newspaper and the inventor of a moustache wax), and line 103.

55   *l'agioteur snob*: We learn what is sold to the snobbish stockbroker at line 60.

56   *Jacob*: Jacob bought his birthright from his starving brother Esau for bread and a pottage of lentils (Genesis 25:29–34).

Footnote 1, line 1 *Même est-on sûr*: From here to the end of the poem Roussel makes extensive use of footnotes. Sixty-two of Canto III's 172 lines and 134 of Canto IV's 232 lines are in footnotes.

A parrot on its perch seemingly
talking to a passer-by. No
other people. (lines 38–39)

Un franc snob que gonfla l'achat d'un droit d'aînesse
Qu' Esaü pleura, snob lui-même, en digérant;))))

Que peser le soleil, asservir la vapeur,

Faire d'un ciel son but et ressentir la peur

D'un séjour encombré de flammes éternelles   5

Ou, s'il parle, sortir des phrases personnelles,

Entre un quidam et lui, pourtant, que de rapports!

Ne retrouvons-nous pas nos instincts chez les porcs?

Chez les chiens sauveteurs qui foncent à la nage?),

Décréta que de l'homme il serait l'apanage?   10

Gageons que le mulet (monture de combat

Le cheval plus que l'âne est noble; au lieu du bât,

C'est la mitraille, lui, qui, par devant, le blesse;

Et tout dans son aspect signale sa noblesse,

Alors qu'on est moins sûr, dans le tas des humains,   15

De reconnaître au port, à la blancheur des mains,

L'individu qu'écrase un nom à particule

Que:—l'instable ataxique à son pas ridicule

Qui fait sur son chemin s'emporter les roquets;

—Le noyeur de soucis qui chez les mastroquets,   20

Coude léger, front lourd, à grands coups s'intoxique

A son souffle, à son pas ((comme notre ataxique)),

A la clarté de son horizontal jet fort;

—Un génie immense à surnaturel apport

A l'historique affront qu'à son aube il essuie   25

An open snob, swelled by the purchase of a birthright
Which Esau, a snob himself, cried over as he digested his meal;))))

Than to weigh the sun, enslave steam to their will,

Make the sky into their heavenly goal and feel fear

At the prospect of dwelling forever in hell's flames,

Or, should the animal be able to talk, bring out personal phrases,

Yet how many similarities there are between man and beast!

Do we not rediscover our own instincts in pigs?

In life-saving dogs when they plunge into the water?),

Decreed it to be an attribute only of mankind?

We can be pretty certain that the mule (as a mount in warfare

The horse is nobler than the donkey; it's not a packsaddle

That wounds him, but a machine gun, and head on;

And everything in his appearance signals his nobility,

Whereas one can be less sure, among a mass of people,

Of recognizing by his bearing, or by his hands' whiteness,

An individual whom a noble name crushes

Than:—the unstable ataxic by his ridiculous way of walking

Which, as he proceeds, infuriates mongrels;

—The drowner of cares who, in pubs and bars,

With a light elbow and a heavy forehead, gets swiftly drunk,

By his breath, by his gait ((which is just like our ataxic's)),

And by the clearness of his strong horizontal jet;

—A colossal genius, one whose contributions verge on the supernatural,

By the legendary insults he encountered in his youth

Footnote 1 (from previous page), line 13 *C'est la mitraille*: Roussel was throughout the First World War a soldier of the *deuxième classe* in the 13th Vincennes artillery regiment, based in Châlons. Being 37 at the outbreak of the war, he was not required to take part in active combat in the front line. (For more on his career in the army, see *RR*, pp. 189–95, and *RD*, pp. 138–40).

Footnote 1, line 18 *Que*: This list presents eight examples of people who can be more easily recognized from their characteristics or behavior or appearance than the person crushed by a noble name can be distinguished from the *hoi polloi* by his gait or white hands.

A tourist mounted on a mule whose
bridle is held by a muleteer in the
costume of an inhabitant of the
mountains. All seen from the front.
(footnote 1, line 11)

Fut, est et jusqu'au bout sera prépondérant;)))
Des tableaux dont il faut lui seriner l'école;   60
Soit qu'on fonde un journal, soit qu'on lance une colle
Apte—dit l'étiquette—à forcer au besoin

Avant de faire école et de passer messie;
   —A son sang lorsqu'il crache, à ses mollets de coq
L'homme aux prises avec le bacille de Koch;
   —A sa bouche lippue où trempe un nez d'élite
Flanqué d' yeux au bord rouge un pur israélite;   30
   —Au pli de son masque un penseur;—au remuement
Par quoi le contredit son nez l'homme qui ment;
   —A leur sinistre anneau les victimes du maire;)
Souffre de ce qu'on ait mésallié:—sa mère
(En qui son double aspect, même s'il la surprend   35
((Quand, sous un soleil fier des points qu'au nôtre il rend,
En ces pays à sieste où l'on ignore l'âtre,
La femme a, blanche ou noire, un rejeton mulâtre,
Est-elle, s'il s'endort, moins prompte à parler bas,
Moins tremblante, plus tard, en surveillant ses pas,   40
Quand, rieur, il commence à trouver l'équilibre?)),
Ne paralyse pas cette sublime fibre
Qu'excita Salomon lors de son jugement)
S'il eut pour premier gîte un ventre de jument;
   —Son père l'étalon si sa mère est ânesse.   45

Was, is, and always will be a leading one;)))
Paintings belonging to a school whose name must be drummed into
   him;
Whether one founds a newspaper, whether one launches a wax
Capable—so claims the label—of compelling

Before founding a school and being deemed a messiah;
—By the blood in his spit, by his calves like a cock's,
The man battling with Koch's bacillus;
—By his thick-lipped mouth towards which dips a nose of the chosen race,
Flanked by red-rimmed eyes, a pure Israelite;
—By the wrinkle in his features, a thinker;—by the moving
Of his nose, which contradicts him, the man who lies;
—By their wedding rings, worn on the left hand, the victims of the Mayor;)
Suffers because of whoever made the misalliance:—his mother
(In whom his double aspect, even if it surprises her
((When, under a sun proud of its superiority to ours
In those countries where siestas are taken and no one knows about fireplaces,
A woman, either black or white, has a half-caste offspring,
Is she, if he's sleeping, any less concerned to speak softly,
Any less anxious, when, later, watching his first steps,
He laughingly begins to discover how to walk upright?)),
Does not paralyze that sublime natural instinct
That Solomon excited when he came to make his judgment)
If he had as his first resting place the womb of a mare;
His stallion father if his mother is a she-ass.

Footnote 1 (continuing), line 28 *le bacille de Koch*: The tuberculosis bacillus was discovered by Robert Koch in 1882.

Footnote 1, line 29 *A sa bouche lippue*: See note to line 12 of footnote beginning at line 28 of Canto I.

Footnote 1, line 34 *Souffre de ce qu'on ait mésallié*: This returns us to the overarching theme of the footnote, which is whether God made animals snobs, as well as men. It picks up from line 11, "*Gageons que le mulet*": "We can be sure that the mule" suffers as a result of his hybrid parentage; the fault was his mother's if she was a mare and his father was a donkey (lines 34 and 44), or his father's if he was a stallion, and his mother was a she-ass (line 45).

Footnote 1, line 43 *Salomon*: A reference to the judgment of Solomon (1 Kings 3:16–28); the "*sublime fibre*" (line 42) is the maternal instinct of the real mother of the disputed baby.

A thinker's head (the head only).
A wrinkle between his eyebrows.
(footnote 1, line 31)

(((((*Lire* souvent égale *être leurré*, témoin:
—Les chèques faux, payés sans délais ni manières;
—Ce que sert ((((sans avoir poussé plus loin qu'Asnières))))   65
Sur les traits que les noirs trempent dans du poison,
L'anneau qui de leur nez traverse la cloison
Ou leurs déserts sans fin, si vides qu'à la lettre
On n'en tirerait pas un caillou bon à mettre
Contre les dents du fond d'un futur orateur,   70
Dans ses *Impressions* le faux explorateur,
Qui (((((faisant alterner l'aimable et le sévère
Comme il est ordonné dans un vers qu'on révère)))),
Lorsqu'il place un hors-d'œuvre hydrologique ardu
Sur tel grand fleuve auprès duquel un drap tordu   75
Semblerait n'engendrer qu'une larme par terre
Et l'Europe n'avoir pour principale artère
((((Bien qu'il s'agisse là du Danube)))) qu'un ru,
Fait suivre, sans souffler, d'un renseignement cru
Sur les rapports qu'entre eux ont l'amour et le lucre   80
Dans les lieux riverains civilisés ((((le sucre
Ote le goût laissé par un remède amer;))))
Le bouquet, à savoir qu'à ses bouches la mer
Est sur un champ immense exempte de salure;
—Quand passe un faux aveugle à convaincante allure,   85

((((*To read* often equals *to be tricked*, for example:
—False checks, cashed without delay or reluctance;
—That composed (((((though its author has never gone further than
    Asnières))))
On the arrows which blacks steep in poison,
On the rings inserted through the septums of their noses
Or their endless deserts that are literally so empty
One could not find there a single pebble that might be put
Against the back teeth of a future orator,
In the *Impressions* written by a false explorer,
Who ((((making the agreeable and the harsh alternate
As is prescribed in a much-revered verse)))),
Having placed as an hors d'œuvre a strenuous hydrological
Account of some great river in comparison with which a wrung-out
    sheet
Would seem to produce no more than a falling tear
And which makes Europe seem to have for its principal waterway
((((Even though it's the Danube that's in question here)))) a mere
    channel,
And followed that up, without pause for breath, with a set of crude
    facts
About the relationship between love and money that pertains
In places along the riverbank that have been civilized ((((sugar
Takes away the taste left by a bitter medicine)))),
Would have us know, as his finishing piece, that at this river's mouth
    the sea
Is completely free of salt over an immense area;
—When a fake blind person walks by in a convincing manner,

63   *(((*Lire *souvent égale* être leurré, *témoin*: There follow six examples of occasions when to read is to be deceived. Roussel's use here of the singular *témoin* is referred to in his *Contre-Erratum* (see note to Canto II, line 509).

65   *Asnières*: Asnières-sur-Seine is on the outskirts of Paris.

70   *un futur orateur*: The Ancient Greek orator and statesman Demosthenes (384–322 BC) improved his oratory by practising speaking with a pebble in his mouth.

71   *Dans ses* Impressions *le faux explorateur*: In "Comment j'ai écrit certains de mes livres" Roussel writes: "It is also important that I mention here a rather curious fact. I have travelled a great deal. Notably, in 1920–21, I travelled around the world by way of India, Australia, New Zealand, the Pacific archipelagos, China, Japan, and America . . . I already knew the principal countries of Europe, Egypt and all of North Africa, and later I visited Constantinople, Asia Minor, and Persia. Now, from all these travels I never took a single thing for my books. It seems to me that this is worth pointing out, since it illustrates so clearly how everything in my works derives from the imagination" (*CJ*, p. 27). The false explorer, on the other hand, writes what looks like an authentic travel book without leaving home.

A bank cashier paying a man
the amount due on a check that
he has presented. (line 64)

L'écriteau bref qui s'offre à l'œil apitoyé;
—L'impur certificat du docteur soudoyé;
—Le cadran du compas quand l'aiguille s'affole
Et l'étiquette, enfin, que porte une fiole . . .
Que de tristes produits, en effet, exaltés   90
Par l'inventeur ((((qui, dur, traite de saletés[1]
Les composés rivaux d'espèce similaire)))),

1. Une chose, en son genre, est rarement unique
   Comme, en le leur, jadis, le furent:—la tunique
   Qu'eut, Déjanire aidant, Hercule après Nessus;
   —Chez les simples humains l'insigne processus
   (Qui d'autre eut jamais l'heur de se sentir en vie   5
   Après avoir, rigide, aux corbeaux fait envie?)
   Du mal dont maints témoins virent Lazare atteint;
   —L'effet qu'eut du poisson sur un regard éteint
   Quand, Raphaël présent, fut opéré Tobie;
   —L'effort que la nature, oubliant sa phobie,   10
   Fit en laissant (jamais l'Écriture ne ment)
   Un vide étroit couper en deux spontanément
   La mer qui d'Israël rompait l'essor;—la halte
   Qu'un soir, au seuil de l'heure où sa splendeur exalte
   Ceux qui par le génie ont le front bossué,   15
   Le fougueux soleil fit pour servir Josué;
   —L'or qu'eut certain bélier pour système pilaire.

The brief notice that is presented to the pitying eye;
—The false certificate of illness from the bribed doctor;
—The dial of a compass when the needle's in a spin,
And the label, finally, carried on a flask . . .
How many sad products, in truth, exalted
By their inventors ((((who harshly dismiss as trashy rubbish[1]
Rival compounds of a similar kind)))),

1. A thing is rarely unique of its kind
   In the manner in which, in the old days, were:—the tunic
   Which, with Deianira's help, Hercules had from Nessus;
   —Among mortals, the remarkable transformation
   (Who else has ever had the happiness of feeling alive
   After rigor mortis has made him attractive food for crows?)
   Achieved by Lazarus, which many witnesses saw;
   —The effect a fish had on an extinguished power of sight
   When, with Raphael present, Tobit was operated upon;
   —The effort that nature, forgetting her phobia,
   Made when she allowed (Scripture never lies)
   A narrow gap spontaneously to cut in two
   The sea that was interrupting the flight of the Israelites;—the pause
   That, one evening, on the threshold of the hour when its splendor exalts
   Those whose foreheads are embossed with the star of genius,
   The fiery sun made to help Joshua;
   —The gold that a certain ram had for its fleece.

91　*l'inventeur*: Roussel was himself something of an inventor, on September 18, 1922 filing for a patent for a method of insulation based on the principle of the vacuum. The patent was issued, and a prototype of a vacuum-insulated dwelling built in one of the garages on his property at Neuilly. No commercial manufacture of this invention, however, followed. For further details, see *RD*, pp. 156–58.

Footnote 1, line 2 *la tunique*: A story told by, among others, Ovid (in his *Metamorphoses,* Book IX, lines 98–238). Nessus was a centaur who attempted to kidnap Deianira, newly married to Hercules, while they were crossing a river. Outraged, Hercules shot the centaur with an arrow tipped with poison from the seven-headed snake, the Hydra. Before he died Nessus falsely told Deianira that his blood- and poison-soaked tunic would serve to keep Hercules's love for her alive. After Hercules began an affair with Iole, Deianira gave the tunic to his servant Lichas to give to her errant husband; when he put it on the Hydra's poison so seared his flesh that he built his own funeral pyre, and flung himself on it.

Footnote 1, line 8 *l'effet qu'eut du poisson*: A story from the Book of Tobit (Apocrypha). During a journey that the blind Tobit's son, Tobias, made with the archangel Raphael, he was attacked by, but then caught, a huge fish; Raphael instructed him to save the fish's innards, and on their return to Nineveh Tobias used the gall to cure his father's blindness.

Footnote 1, line 12 *Un vide étroit*: i.e., the space between the walls of water during the parting of the Red Sea.

Footnote 1, line 13 *la halte*: A reference to the battle of Gibeon, at which Joshua asked God to make the sun stand still so the Israelites could complete their defeat of the Amorites (Joshua 10:12–14).

Footnote 1, line 17 *certain bélier*: i.e., the ram whose golden fleece was sought by Jason and the Argonauts.

A man seated at a laid table reading the
label on a phial of medicine. (line 89)

Bien que, passés ou frais, ils agissent non plus
Que:—sur la masse un nom de chantre aux vers peu lus;
—L'haleine du soufflet quand tout est mort dans l'âtre;   95
—Sur un membre de bois le plus actif emplâtre;
—Sur le regard, quand l'œil est artificiel,
Un doigt de belladone;))) à menacer le ciel
(((Menace vaine, on sait que l'astre le plus proche
Loge encore trop haut pour que rien le décroche;)))   100
La moustache rebelle à quoi nul coup de fer
N'ôte la rage, hélas! de menacer l'enfer;
Soit qu'on prépare une eau—poison dont rien ne sauve
Le microbe sournois chargé de rendre chauve—
Capable d'affamer les vendeurs de cheveux;))   105
Avec le doigt et l'œil fait suivre à ses neveux
Sa stricte volonté, féconde ou saugrenue,
—Ses neveux trépignants, qui, dès qu'il éternue,
Joyeux, rêvent de crêpe et de flux lacrymal;),
De provoquer en soi la détente d'un mal.   110

Although, old or new, they work no better
Than:—on the masses the name of a bard whose verses are little read;
—The breath of the bellows when all is dead in the hearth;
—The most active plaster on a wooden leg;
—On the sight of an artificial eye
A tincture of belladonna;))) to threaten the heavens
(((Vain threat, for we know that the nearest star
Is still too high for anything to unhook it;)))
The recalcitrant moustache, though no grooming,
Alas! can overcome its determination to threaten hell instead;
Or whether one prepares a solution—a poison from which nothing
    can save
The sly microbe that renders men bald—
That will one day reduce to starvation those who sell hair;))
With finger and eye makes his nephews follow
His exact wishes, whether productive or preposterous,
—His nephews, wracked with anticipation, who, when he sneezes,
Dream joyfully of mourning armbands and flowing tears;),
Of bringing about the easing of one's pain.

94   *Que*: This list consists of four things that don't work. Given Roussel's extravagant hopes for his own œuvre, there is a certain pathos in the first illustration offered ("*sur la masse un nom de chantre aux vers peu lus*"). "I shall reach immense heights," Roussel assured the psychologist Pierre Janet, who wrote up his case in *De l'angoisse à l'extase* (1926), "and am destined for blazing glory . . . This glory will be evident in every one of my works, and will reflect on all the acts of my life; people will research the way I played prisoners' base. No author has been or ever can be greater than I, although no one is aware of this yet today. Well, what can you expect—there are some shells which explode with great difficulty, but when they do explode! . . . Whatever you may think, there are some who are predestined!" His conviction of his literary greatness was accompanied by specific physical symptoms; during the composition of *La Doublure* he records feeling "the equal of Dante and Shakespeare":

> Whatever I wrote was surrounded by rays of light; I used to close the curtains, for I was afraid that the shining rays emanating from my pen might escape into the outside world through even the smallest chink; I wanted suddenly to throw back the screen and light up the world. To leave these papers lying about would have sent out rays of light as far as China, and the desperate crowd would have flung themselves upon my house. But it was in vain I took such precautions, for rays of light were streaming from me and through the walls, I was carrying the sun within myself and could do nothing to impede the tremendous light I was radiating. Each line was repeated in thousands of copies, and I wrote with a thousand flaming pen-nibs. Without a doubt, when the volume appeared, this blinding furnace would be revealed and would illuminate the entire universe, but what no one would believe was that I was carrying it all along within myself. (*De l'angoisse à l'extase*, reprinted in *CJ*, pp. 128–30)

98   *à menacer le ciel*: This returns to the inventor of the moustache wax of lines 61–62: its label claims it is able to force up the points of one's moustache so high that they threaten the sky.

106   *Avec le doigt et l'œil*: this picks up from line 6 and the "*oncle d'Amérique.*"

110   *De provoquer en soi la détente d'un mal*: This completes the opening syntactic unit interrupted at line 5.

A nocturnal landscape. Very
starry sky with a thin crescent
moon. No people. (lines 99–100)

IV

Les Jardins de Rosette vus d'une dahabieh

ENVIRONS DU CAIRE

Rasant le Nil, je vois fuir deux rives couvertes
De fleurs, d'ailes, d'éclairs, de riches plantes vertes
Dont une suffirait à vingt de nos salons
(Doux salons où sitôt qu'ont tourné deux talons
((En se divertissant soit de sa couardise   5
(((Force particuliers, quoi qu'on leur fasse ou dise,
Jugeant le talion d'un emploi peu prudent,
Rendent salut pour œil et sourire pour dent;)))
Si—fait aux quolibets transparents, à la honte—
(((Se fait-on pas à tout? deux jours après la tonte,   10
Le mouton aguerri ne ressent plus le frais;

IV

The Gardens of Rosetta seen from a dahabieh

OUTSKIRTS OF CAIRO

Skimming the Nile, I see flitting by two banks covered
With flowers, with wings, with flashes of brightness, with rich green
    plants
Of which one could provide twenty of our salons
(Sweet salons, where as soon as someone has turned on his heels and
    left
((Amusing themselves with talk either of his cowardice
(((Many individuals, whatever one does or says to them,
Judging retaliation an imprudent course of action,
Return a greeting for an eye and a smile for a tooth;)))
If—having grown shamefully accustomed to open jibes—
((((Do we not get used to anything? Two days after being sheared
The sheep is inured and no longer feels the cold;

Les Jardins de Rosette: Rosetta or Rashid is a village on the banks of the western arm of the Nile once famous for its gardens and date palm plantations. The Rosetta Stone was found there in 1799. It is not on the outskirts of Cairo.

une dahabieh: A houseboat used on the Nile.

1   *je*: This is the only time Roussel himself appears in the poem.

3   *nos salons*: Turn to the last line of the canto (98) to complete this sentence.

4   *deux talons*: Turn to the canto's penultimate line (97) to complete this Proustian scene.

9   *à la honte*: This syntactic unit is completed in lines 95 and 96.

10   *(((Se fait-on*: *Fait* in the previous line is the "hook" Roussel uses here to introduce five examples of things that animals (sheep [11] and parrot [13]) and people (an envious person [17], an astronomer [24], and a mute [94]) get used to.

An elegantly dressed man descending the staircase of a luxurious lobby in evening coat and top hat. His open overcoat reveals that he is wearing black. (lines 4 and 97)

S'il peut rire, chanter, siffler, faire des frais,
C'est que le perroquet se fait vite à la chaîne
Qui—lui qui sait vieillir comme vieillit un chêne
Quand nul n'est au persil des mets où son bec mord—   15
Le rive à son perchoir et l'y rivera mort;
L'envieux ((((dont les nuits cessaient de couler calmes
Au vu d'un nom ami dans la liste des palmes
Et chez qui se perdaient le boire et le manger
Quand, non moins célébré qu'en France à l'étranger,   20
Un confrère—à l'en croire une franche savate—
Voyait se transformer sa rosette en cravate))))
Se fait au sentiment du montage d'autrui;
L'astronome ((((tel astre apparaît aujourd'hui
Comme un feu dont l'éclat aux clignements nous force   25
Qui, lorsque l'eau couvrait, de la terrestre écorce,
Tout, sauf les pics par l'homme encore non atteints,
S'était classé déjà dans les mondes éteints . . .
—Tout feu s'éteint, en nous comme dans la nature;
Sur les plis qu'on n'obtient que contre signature   30
D'un souffle l'envoyeur éteint chaque cachet;
L'âge éteint certains feux: jamais las, le cochet
Prend tout, poulette, poule à point, poule douairière . . .
Le coq mûr fait un choix; les poltrons, au derrière,

If it can laugh, sing, whistle, and make an effort to please,
It is because the parrot quickly gets used to the chain
Which—he who is able to grow as old as an old oak tree
As long as no parsley is put in the food his beak pecks at—
Rivets him to his perch, and will rivet him there when he's dead;
The envious type ((((whose nights cease to flow calmly
If he spots the name of a friend in the prize list
And on whom food and drink are wasted
When, no less celebrated abroad than in France,
A colleague—someone he would have you believe is a complete
    bungler—
Sees an honorary rosette become an honorary cravat))))
Gets used to feelings inspired by the rise of others;
The astronomer ((((some star that appears today
Like a fire whose brilliance forces us to blink,
Was, when water covered the earth's entire surface
Except for various peaks that have not yet been climbed by man,
Already in the category of worlds that have been extinguished . . .
—All fires die out, in us as in nature;
On those letters that can be received only with a signature
The sender extinguishes each wax seal by blowing on it;
Age extinguishes certain fires: never tired, the cockerel
Took anything, pullets, grown-up hens, old dowagers . . .
The mature cock makes a careful choice; cowards, in the rear,

15   *persil*: Parsley is widely believed to be toxic to parrots.

22   *sa rosette en cravate*: The difference between an *Officier* and a *Commandeur* in the ranks of those granted a *Légion d'honneur*. Roussel was himself elected *Chevalier* (the lowest grade) on February 14, 1932. This followed a donation he made to the organization of 50,000 francs.

24   *l'astronome*: Turn to lines 92 and 93, and Zo's final illustration, no. 59, to find out what the astronomer gets used to.

29   —*Tout feu s'éteint*: This initiates a list of the different kinds of fire, real and metaphorical, that die out, a list that dominates the main body of the text of this canto.

A snowy, deserted peak that
creates the impression of extreme
altitude and inaccessibility. (line 27)

Ont un feu qui s'abstient de survivre au danger   35
(((((Feu cuisant, mais fictif; jamais, à vidanger,
Nul ne fut intrigué par sa cendre, et le lièvre
Ne le vit pas brusquer les grenouilles;))))); la fièvre
Crée un feu qui s'éteint, soit quand le sujet meurt,
Soit quand, grandi parfois à menacer d'un heurt,   40
Lustres, vos cristaux bas et vos basses ampoules[1],

   1. Tout progresse; au moment où, rendant pour les poules,
       Ces sages couche-tôt, le premier somme urgent,
       Le soleil plonge à l'ouest, même riche (l'argent
       Fait avec lui, de front, marcher le privilège;
       Le cancre chic est sûr d'éclipser au collège   5
       ((Aux dessus du prochain on reconnaît son rang
       Comme:—sa provenance au son suspect ou franc
       Qu'émet une monnaie en sautant sur un marbre;
       —A sa striation l'âge d'un tronçon d'arbre;
       —A sa denture l'an où naquit un coursier;))   10
       L'aigle dont, à l'envi, les coudes de boursier
       D'un proche percement font luire la promesse;
       Au suicidé riche on accorde une messe:
       Il est dur de partir sans un *De profondis*;),
       On portait l'allumette à la mèche jadis,   15
       Geste qu'a fait vieillir l'éclairage électrique;

Have a fire that fails to survive danger
(((((This fire, though burning, is fictitious; none was ever
Intrigued by the ashes it left while cleaning them out, and the hare
Never saw it abruptly abandon the frogs;))))); fever
Creates a fire which goes out, either when the subject dies
Or when, sometimes made tall enough to threaten with a blow,
O chandeliers, the lowest of your crystals and bulbs[1],

1. All things progress; at the moment when, bringing for hens,
   Those wise early-retirers, their urgently needed first sleep,
   The sun sinks in the west, even the rich (money
   Makes privilege march abreast with it;
   The chic dunce is sure to eclipse at college
   ((One can recognize the superiority of his rank to that of his neighbors
   As one can:—its provenance from the sound, suspicious or clear,
   That a coin makes when bounced on marble;
   —From its rings the age of a tree trunk;
   —From its teeth the year that a horse was born;))
   The genius whose worn-out scholarship boy's elbow-patches, to the envy
   Of others, shiningly promise a forthcoming breakthrough;
   To the rich suicide a mass is granted;
   It is hard to depart without a *De Profundis*;),
   Carried, in the old days, a match to a candle wick,
   An act which electric lighting has rendered obsolete;

37   *le lièvre*: A reference to the La Fontaine fable "*Le Lièvre et les gre-nouilles*" ("The Hare and the Frogs"), in which a hare inadvertently startles a colony of cowardly frogs, who dive into a pond for safety.

Footnote 1, line 3, 15 *même riche . . . / On portait l'allumette*: In the old days even rich people had to light candles, but ("*Tout progresse*") electricity means they no longer have to.

Footnote 1, line 4 *le privilège*: Two examples of the privileges granted by wealth are offered: the chic dunce eclipsing at college the poor scholarship boy, and the mass granted a rich suicide (lines 13 and 14, and Zo's illustration).

Footnote 1, line 6 *on reconnaît son rang*: Whereas in the first footnote of Canto III it was declared harder to recognize a noble person than an ataxic or a drunkard or a genius, the rank of the chic dunce is as easy to recognize as . . . (three examples follow).

An elegantly dressed man pointing
the barrel of a revolver to his
temple, his finger on the trigger.
(footnote 1, line 13)

—La fièvre nous fait croître, on le sait, même adultes—
Par degrés il se change en frais convalescent
Poussé par la fringale à manger comme cent
Et porteur d'une langue à nouveau bien rougie;   45
Le feu qui, patient, fait fondre une bougie
S'éteint:—tandis que choit le marteau lorsqu'on vend
Un immeuble à l'encan;—sous un assaut de vent,
Quand, aux flambeaux, l'on sort un roi d'une demeure,
Pompe que l'héritier, qui paierait pour qu'il meure[1],   50

Le moteur, provoquant la baisse sur la trique,
A mis en discrédit le tirage animal,
  —Et depuis les moineaux, pour vivre, ont plus de mal;
Que sont près des canons les gauches catapultes?   20
1. Que de choses se font attendre, hélas! depuis
    Le plongeon du caillou qu'on lâche dans un puits,
    Les hommages publics,—sommité disparue
    Seule est en droit d'avoir sa statue et sa rue,—
    La fin quand dans l'eau froide un bloc de sucre fond,   5
    Pour l'homme sans sommeil ces blancheurs, au plafond,
    Par quoi sont annoncés l'aurore et son spectacle,
    Dans tout feuilleton sain la chute de l'obstacle
    Qui du parfait bonheur sépare le héros,
    L'épouseur quand le sac n'est pas réputé gros,   10
    Le revers de costume à ruban écarlate

—A fever makes us grow, even adults, everyone knows this—
By degrees he turns into a hearty convalescent
Driven by pangs of hunger to eat like a hundred
And the bearer of a tongue that is nicely red again;
The flame that patiently melts a candle
Dies out:—at the moment the hammer falls when a building
Is sold at auction;—under the wind's assault,
When, by torchlight, a king is brought from his residence,
A ceremony that his heir, who would pay to see him dead[1],

The motor, bringing about a decline in the use of the cudgel,
Has put draught animals out of favor,
—And ever since sparrows have had more trouble surviving;
What, in comparison with cannon, are clumsy catapults?

1. How many things there are, alas, that make people wait, such as
The fall of a pebble that one drops down a well,
Public acclaim,—only an eminent person who is dead
Has the right to a statue and a street named after him,—
The end when a lump of sugar is melting in cold water,
For a man who can't sleep, the white patches on the ceiling
That herald the dawn and the spectacle it brings,
In any decent serial the collapse of the obstacle
Which separates the hero from perfect happiness,
The prospective husband when the dowry is said not to be large,
The lapel of a jacket for a scarlet ribbon,

42   *La fièvre nous fait croître*: There is little evidence to support the belief expressed here that fevers make people grow.

47   *S'éteint*: There follow five examples of moments when candles are extinguished, which form a kind of subset of the larger theme of fires going out.

Footnote 1, line 4 *sa rue*: When Roussel eventually sold his property at Neuilly in 1931, he had a clause inserted into the contract stipulating that if ever the land should be developed and a road built through it, that road should be called "avenue Raymond-Roussel." However, no such avenue exists among the network of cooperatives built during the1950s on the plot occupied by 25 boulevard Richard-Wallace.

A walker, with his arm raised and his fingers open, who has just dropped a pebble (which is still visible) down a well, inclining his head as if to listen out for the splash (no other people).

(footnote 1, line 2)

Grille en secret de voir se déployer pour lui[1];

Jusqu'au tonnerre, alors que, sourd, le coup n'éclate
Qu'une minute après qu'un faible éclair a lui!

1. Nul n'est sans caresser un ambitieux rêve;
   L'ouvrier croit se voir dictant, lors d'une grève
   (Aujourd'hui l'on raisonne et chacun, l'œil au but
   ((Tous nous en avons un; tant que son occiput,
   Mis nu dans l'intérêt du fer de la machine,   5
   Tient pour plus d'un quart d'heure encore à son échine,
   Songeant: « Perdre sa proie arrive—et c'est fréquent—
   A qui la tient le mieux » (((au fait, l'inconséquent
   S'enfuit du cabanon, le reclus de la geôle,
   Le fromage du bec du corbeau qu'on enjôle;   10
   —De se taire, parfois, riche est l'occasion;)))
   L'assassin a lui-même un but: l'évasion;)),
   Que son idéal soit: toucher un gros salaire,
   Enfanter, voir son grain surabonder sur l'aire
   Ou contraindre son pouls à choir, à s'assagir,   15
   Sent que, pour triompher, mieux vaut penser, agir
   Que faire—tâcheron, épousée inféconde,
   Moissonneur ou malade—un vœu dans la seconde
   Où l'étoile filante élonge sa lueur;),
   Las de donner à boire au bourgeois sa sueur   20
   (C'est pour Pierre, souvent, que Paul souffre et travaille;
   Vespuce, de Colomb, exploita la trouvaille;

Secretly burns to see deployed on his own account[1];

    And finally the thunder, whose muffled peal breaks only
    A minute after a feeble bolt of lightning has flashed!

1. There is no one who does not cherish an ambitious dream;
    The worker believes he will see himself dictating, at the time of a strike
    (These days people use their reason, and each, with an eye on the goal
    ((We all have one: as long as the nape of his neck,
    Laid bare for the blade of the guillotine,
    Remains for a quarter of an hour longer connected to his spine,
    Thinking: "Letting one's prey slip occurs—often—even
    To someone who holds it most securely" (((and indeed, the imbecile
    Escapes from his padded cell, the prisoner in solitary confinement from his jail,
    The cheese from the beak of the duped crow;
    —On some occasions keeping silent is the best option;))),
    The murderer has only one aim: escape;)),
    Whatever his or her ideal is: to earn a large salary,
    To give birth to children, to see the threshing floor overflowing with his grain
    Or to make his pulse rate slow and settle down,
    Feels that, to succeed, it is better to think and act
    Than to make—jobbing worker, infertile wife,
    Harvester or invalid—a wish in the moment
    That a shooting star leaves its shining trail;),
    Tired of giving his sweat to the bourgeoisie to drink
    (It is often for Peter that Paul suffers and works;
    Vespucci exploited Columbus's discovery;

Footnote 1, line 2 *lors d'une grève*: The ambitious worker's dream is continued at line 20, interrupted again, and completed at line 24.

Footnote 1, line 3 *l'œil au but*: This is picked up at line 13.

Footnote 1, line 10 *le fromage du bec du corbeau*: Another reference to Aesop's fable of "The Fox and the Crow"; see note to Canto II, lines 310–11.

Instructions: Zo's picture of Amerigo Vespucci is indeed very similar to that in the *Nouveau Larousse illustré*.

A portrait (unnamed) of Amerigo Vespucci. You might base the picture on that in the *Nouveau Larousse illustré*. (footnote 1, line 22)

—Quand, brutal, au sortir d'un lointain pistolet
Qu'étreint un champion dont tous les coups font mouche,
Un projectile heureux rompt la mèche ou la mouche;
—Quand un liseur, au lit (((((dos hors de l'oreiller,   55
Front en main, tant il sent l'intérêt s'éveiller))))),
Dévore justement quelque poignant passage
Où, mère sans anneau (((((que l'univers croit sage
Tant son accouchement sut être clandestin)))))
Dont (((((prêt à joindre au sien son plantureux destin)))))   60
S'est épris pour la vie un banquier de la haute,
Une jeune employée, un an après la faute[1],

Et c'est pour emperler tel doigt ou tel plastron
Qu'une huître est tout labeur;), des lois à son patron;
La garce en son grenier pense à rouler carrosse;   25
Se voir pousser aux mains l'améthyste et la crosse
Est une fiction chère à tout prestolet.

1. Combien change de force un mot suivant les cas!
Éclair dit « feu du ciel escorté de fracas »
Ou « reflet qu'un canif fait jaillir de sa lame »;
Corbeille qui, trouvé dans un épithalame,
Offre aux yeux de l'esprit l'empire du joyau   5
Rend ailleurs « dépotoir à vieux papiers »; *noyau*
Ici sert pour « comète » et sert là pour « cerise »;

—When, on brutally leaving a distant pistol
That's in the grip of a champion whose every shot hits the bull's-eye,
A bullet successfully strikes the candle's wick or snuff;
When a reader, in bed (((((his back off the pillow
And with his forehead in his hand, so strongly is his interest
   awakened))))),
Justly devours a certain poignant passage
In which an unmarried mother (((((whom the world still believes
   well-behaved,
So secretly was her confinement managed)))))
With whom (((((ready to join to hers his prosperous future)))))
A highly placed banker has fallen in love for life,
This young employee, a year after she committed her fault[1],

---

And it is to furnish a pearl for some finger or waistcoat
That an oyster spends its life laboring;), laws to his boss;
The slut in her attic dreams of living in style;
And to see his hands adorned with amethysts and holding a crozier
Is a fantasy dear to each fledgling priest.
1. How a word changes its meaning according to its context!
   Éclair means "fire in the sky accompanied by loud noise"
   Or "the reflection that a penknife makes flash from its blade";
   Corbeille, if found in an epithalamium,
   Presents to the mind's eye the world of gems
   But becomes elsewhere "a place to deposit old papers"; *noyau*
   Can be used here in relation to a "comet" and there to a "cherry";

54   *la mouche*: A contraction, for the rhyme's sake, of *mouchure*, meaning the snuff or burned portion of a candle's wick.

Footnote 1, line 1 *Combien change de force un mot*: What Roussel called his "*procédé très spécial*" (his very special method), which he revealed only in the posthumously published essay "Comment j'ai écrit certains de mes livres," is based on the fact that words have more than one meaning. In this essay he explains:

> I would choose a word and then link it to another by the preposition *à*; and these two words, when considered in relation to meanings other than their initial meaning, supplied me with a further creation . . . I will cite some examples . . . 1st *baleine* (a whale) *à îlot* (a small island) 2nd *baleine* (corset whalebone) *à ilote* (a helot or Spartan slave);* 1st *duel* (a combat between two people) *à accolade* (an embrace, as when two adversaries, reconciled after the duel, embrace each other); 2nd *duel* (the dual tense in a Greek verb) *à accolade* (typographical bracket); 1st *mou* (a feeble individual) *à raille* (here I thought of the raillery heaped on a lazy student by his comrades); 2nd *mou* (the culinary dish made from the lungs of a calf) *à rail* (railway line). These last three groups of words gave me the statue of the helot sculpted from corset whalebones rolling on rails made of calf's lights and bearing on its base an inscription relating to the dual form of a Greek verb.

> *There was occasionally a slight difference between the words as here, for example, where *îlot* differs a little from *ilote*.

Roussel felt it to be his duty to explain this special method to posterity, believing it might prove useful for later writers, but he didn't want it known while he was alive. He even records altering one formulation, fearing it might lead to his secret being exposed. This footnote is the closest he got to suggesting the existence of the *procédé* in the writings he published during his lifetime.

Footnote 1, line 2 *Éclair*: lightning/flash.

Footnote 1, line 4 *Corbeille*: wedding presents given to bride by bridegroom/wastepaper basket.

Footnote 1, line 6 *noyau*: nucleus of a comet/stone of a cherry.

A man, bust only, in profile
(right profile) aiming at something
with a pistol (one cannot see what he is
aiming at). (lines 52–53)

Apprête son enfant pour un furtif baptême
Qui n'alourdira pas, hélas! un seul drageoir,
Si, pour rire, quelqu'un planta dans le bougeoir 65
Une bougie-attrape invisiblement faite

A *révolution* peut correspondre « crise
Où du prince obéi le peuple dit: Je veux »
Ou « court ébranlement d'un système nerveux »; 10
De « fauteuil » saute à « mer » *bras*; de « tome » à « roi » *suite*;
De « façon dont croupit l'homme » à « tuyau » *conduite*;
De « grinçant cube en craie » à « civilisé » *blanc*;
D' « écueil traître où la mort plane » à « siège ingrat » *banc*;
« Manger louche » ou « support chic » de *champignon* use; 15
« Ce dont s'arme un gêneur à marteau qu'on excuse »
Ou « numéro suant le prestige » est dans *clou*;
« Ce qui, le décrassage aidant, rend le bain flou »
Dans *savon* ou « ce qu'un chauffé sous-ordre écoute »;
« Affliction qu'hostile au somme un péché coûte » 20
Ou « mèche à chatouiller le cou » dans *repentir*;
« Trait par quoi dès l'enfance on s'exerce à mentir »
Dans *bâton* ou « suprême attribut militaire »;
« Emplumé rôtisseur d'humains propriétaire
D'un arc » dans *naturel* ou « simple heureux défaut 25
D'apprêt »; dans *paradis* « puant cintre » ou « Là-Haut,
Bien habité séjour fleuri rendant les justes
Choristes »; « timbale à tralala pour robustes

Readies her child for a furtive baptism
That will not, alas, involve filling up a single sweet box,
If, for a laugh, someone planted in the candlestick
A hoax candle impossible to detect

Révolution can represent "crisis
In which the people say to the prince they obeyed: 'We want'"
Or "a brief shuddering of the nervous system";
From "armchair" to "sea" the word *bras* can jump; from "volume" to "king" *suite*;
From "a lazy life that man leads" to "pipe," *conduite*;
From "a cube of chalk to grind on a billiard cue" to "civilized," *blanc*;
From "treacherous reef where death hovers" to "unpleasing seat," *banc*;
"A suspect food" or "chic support" are both in *champignon*;
"That with which an intruder with a hammer, whom one excuses, is armed"
Or "number exuding prestige" is in *clou*;
"That which, an aid to cleaning, makes the bath murky"
In *savon* or "that which a hot-faced subordinate hears";
"Affliction caused by a sin that is hostile to sleep"
Or "tress that tickles the neck" in *repentir*;
"Pen stroke with which from childhood one practices lying"
In *bâton* or "supreme military attribute";
"Feather-wearing roaster of human beings and the owner
Of a bow" in *naturel* or "simple happy lack
Of affectation"; in *paradis* "high stinking gallery in the theatre" or "up above,
A well-inhabited flower-strewn resort where the just become
Choristers"; "a fancy dish for robust

Footnote 1 (from previous page), line 8 *révolution*: political revolution/revulsion.

Footnote 1, line 11 *bras*: arm of an armchair/a maritime sound or coastal inlet.

Footnote 1, line 11 *suite*: retinue/sequel.

Footnote 1, line 12 *conduite*: behavior/piping.

Footnote 1, line 13 *blanc*: cube of billiard chalk/white man. This pun is crucial to the evolution of Roussel's first story, "Parmi les noirs" ("Among the Blacks"), and the *procédé* that then developed out of it. See *CJ*, pp. 11–12.

Footnote 1, line 14 *banc*: sandbank/bench.

Footnote 1, line 15 *champignon* mushroom/milliner's hat-stand.

Footnote 1, line 17 *clou*: nail/star turn or show's highlight performance. The excused intruder with a hammer of the previous line is a workman carrying out indoor repairs.

Footnote 1, line 19 *savon*: soap/dressing-down.

Footnote 1, line 21 *repentir*: repentance/ringlet of hair.

Footnote 1, line 23 *bâton*: stroke of a pen/a field marshal's baton.

Footnote 1, line 25 *naturel*: primitive/not artificial.

Footnote 1, line 26 *paradis*: the Gods in a theatre/heaven.

A stone bench, without a backrest,
surrounded by trees. No people.
(footnote 1, line 14)

Pour ne pouvoir brûler plus avant que son faîte[1];

Gasters » ou « pleur de plume incongru » dans *pâté*;
« Scientifique choix d'aliments à gâté   30
Plaisir » dans *régime* ou « façon dont on se laisse
Par la clique au pouvoir tondre et mener en laisse »;
« Cri par quoi, l'un soufflant l'autre, un *alter ego*
Vous raille » ou « paragraphe influent » dans *écho*;
Faute enfin peint l'écart qui fait qu'est *avec tache*   35
Celle qu'on ne *voit* plus ou l'impair qu'un potache
A tel endroit précis commit dans son devoir;
Or, décidera-t-on, lui, de ne plus le voir
Parce qu'un barbarisme est éclos dans son thème?

1. Tour que valent ceux-ci, quant à l'attrait du neuf:
Faire indûment couver par une poule un œuf
Dont l'autour avéré n'est autre qu'une cane,
Pour voir trembler la poule (autour de qui cancane,
Cherchant à quel canard elle fit trop la cour,   5
Bas, le bec demi-clos, toute la basse-cour)
Dès que le caneton s'humecte la cheville;
Cultiver la terreur chez une vieille fille
(Une au cœur faible en qui le goût du célibat
Fut formé par la peur du mari saoul qui bat   10
Ou l'exemple fameux du veuf à barbe bleue)
En affublant son chat d'un brandon à la queue
Propre à le faire fuir vers elle éperdument.

That prevents it burning beyond its tip[1];

Digestions" or "unseemly tear from one's pen" in *pâté*;
"Scientific choice of foods designed to spoil
Pleasure" in *régime* or "manner in which one allows
The clique in power to clip and lead one on a leash";
"Cry by which, one mimicking the other, an alter ego
Mocks you" or "influential paragraph" in *écho*;
And finally *faute* describes the transgression which means one no longer
Sees someone who is ruined or the mistake that a schoolboy
Makes at a precise point in his homework;
Now, would one decide no longer to see this schoolboy
Merely because a barbarism is clearly visible in his prose?

1. A trick, as far as novelty goes, equalled by these:
To make a hen improperly sit on an egg
That has in fact been laid by a duck,
In order to see the hen tremble (while around her the entire poultry yard
Engages in gossip, trying to find out which drake she courted too freely,
Bending low, beaks half-closed),
As soon as the duckling gets its ankles wet;
To terrify an old woman
(One with a weak heart in whom the taste for celibacy
Was formed by fear of a drunken, wife-beating husband
Or the famous example of Bluebeard)
By rigging her cat out with a torch on its tail
That makes it flee towards her distractedly.

Footnote 1 (continuing), line 29 *pâté*: pâté/blob of ink.
Footnote 1, line 31 *régime*: diet/political regime.
Footnote 1, line 34 *écho*: echo/literary influence.
Footnote 1, line 35 *faute*: transgression/mistake.
67   *son faîte*: The progress saluted in the canto's first footnote, which makes candles obsolete, seems not to have reached the unlucky victim of this hoax candle.

A man in a mountainous spot cupping
his ear as if to better hear an echo.
(footnote 1, lines 33–34)

—Lorsque part dans son sens un brusque éternuement
Suivi de vœux faits haut pour voir par Dieu bénie
La personne au nez pris; le saint feu du génie   70
(((((Qui rend l'élu touché par lui si vaniteux
Qu'il trouve au firmament les vrais astres piteux
Auprès de l'astre neuf qui sur son front rayonne
Et songe à devenir le maître que crayonne
Quiconque a pour métier l'art caricatural,   75
—Art né, dit-on, un soir, du fou profil mural
Qu'offrait à des rieurs l'ombre d'une personne,—
A la porte duquel maint journaliste sonne,
Qui sur vingt grands cordons existants en tient un,
Lui qui souvent, alors qu'il se couche, est à jeun   80
Non moins que le fidèle en qui descend l'hostie[1])))))

1. Si le mérite humain exclut la modestie
        Autant que le lundi l'ardeur des travailleurs
        (On se fait aux loisirs; l'âme et le cœur ailleurs,
        Sombre est le lycéen quand il rentre en octobre;),
        Que, chez le criminel, la démence l'opprobre,   5
        Qu'un hiver peu neigeux la cherté du gros sel,
        L'orgueil, pourtant, n'est pas un vice universel;
        Le paon mis en dehors, il respecte les bêtes:

—When a sneeze is suddenly made in its direction
Followed by loud wishes to see blessed by God
The person with the afflicted nose; the holy fire of genius
(((((Which makes the elect one touched by it so vain
That he finds the real stars in the sky pitiful
In comparison with the new star that shines on his forehead
And dreams of becoming a master who is sketched
By anyone who has the job of being a caricaturist,
—An art born, it is said, one evening, from the crazy profile on a wall
That the shadow of somebody presented to those laughing at it,—
At whose door numerous journalists ring,
And who holds one of the twenty most important ribbons of honor
    there are,
He who often, when he goes to bed, is to fasting
As faithful as the believer who has just swallowed the host[1])))))

1. If human excellence drives out modesty
    As much as Monday does the ardor of workers
    (One gets used to leisure; the soul and the heart elsewhere,
    The *lycée* pupil is sombre when he returns in October;),
    And insanity, in the case of a criminal, the shame of his crime,
    And an unsnowy winter high prices for road salt,
    Yet pride is not a universal vice;
    Leaving aside the peacock, it steers clear of beasts:

73 *l'astre neuf qui sur son front rayonne*: "Whatever you may think," Roussel told Janet, "there are some who are predestined! As the poet says [Roussel himself]: *et voilà qu'on se sent une brûlure au front ... L'étoile qu'on porte au front resplendissante* [And there are those who feel a burning on their forehead ... The star which they carry on their shining brow]. Yes, I have felt that I too carry a star on my forehead, and I will never forget it" (*CJ*, p. 128). In the last scene of his 1924 play *L'Étoile au front* Roussel has the character Joussac describe a work by one Boissenin entitled *Prédestinés*. Boissenin's thesis, Joussac explains,

> turns on a poetic image: that of *the star on the forehead*, — which certain people have from birth, but no one ever acquires; it's the sublime mark of great creators in all the various branches of the arts. Unwavering in his belief that divine and all-powerful innate gifts are distributed randomly, he shows the odd manner in which, throughout the ages and from top to bottom of the social scale, these stars have been allocated. He compares numerous wonderful careers accomplished against the odds with the wretched achievements of mediocrities who happen to have the wind in their sails! Here, one of the elect, misunderstood by all around him—who try to defeat him by starving him—defies misery to attain his goal; there, another, who could have lived an idle life, gives to the world a strange example of relentless hard work and manly fortitude.

The immensely wealthy, furiously industrious Roussel clearly has himself in mind in this last example.

80 *à jeun*: Fearing that eating would damage his "serenity," Roussel used to fast for days, then gorge himself on cakes at the famous cake shop, Rumpelmeyer's.

A man on a landing in the act of
ringing a doorbell. (line 78)

S'éteint quand l'âge rend son détenteur gaga
(((((Feu qui, si grand que soit tel nom, tel pseudonyme,
Chez nul n'est reconnu de façon unanime;
—L'homme n'a pas ainsi qu'un pantin au bazar   85
Son prix collé sur lui;))))); sur son mur Balthazar
Vit, en traits défiant le grattoir et la gomme,
Trois mots de feu briller . . . puis s'éteindre; chez l'homme,
Le feu de l'œil s'éteint à l'âge où dent par dent
Et cheveu par cheveu, sans choc, sans accident,   90

L'hirondelle, malgré son flair pour les tempêtes;
Le bélier, bien qu'il soit l'emblème d'un crachat   10
(Tout le monde a nommé la Toison d'Or); le chat,
Bien qu'il se reconnaisse à minuit sans chandelle,
Bien qu'il sache prédire—ainsi que l'hirondelle,
Mais sans tant de justesse et de publicité—
Par ce qu'émet son poil comme électricité   15
La colère d'un ciel qui feint la gentillesse,
Bien qu'à la vierge il fasse une douce vieillesse
Et puisse marcher en silence sans tapis;
Le loup, bien qu'une louve ait eu d'illustres pis;
Le bouc, bien qu'aux humains sa peau fournisse l'outre;   20
Malgré les prix courants de la sienne, la loutre;
Bien que son nom désigne un tissu, l'alpaga.

Is extinguished when old age renders its possessor gaga
(((((A fire which, however great the genius's name or pseudonym,
Has never been recognized unanimously;
—A man's gifts are no more than a puppet at the bazaar,
With its price stuck on it;))))); on his wall Belshazzar
Saw, in writing no scraper or eraser could efface,
Three words shine brilliantly in fire . . . then fade; with men
The fire in the eye goes out at the age when tooth by tooth
And hair by hair, without shock or accident,

The swallow, despite its ability to predict tempests;

The ram, although it is the emblem of the order of the Grand Cross

(Everyone is familiar with the Golden Fleece); the cat,

Although it can work out its bearings at midnight without a candle,

Although it knows how to predict—just like the swallow,

But not so accurately or publicly—

By the static its fur gives off

The anger lurking in a sky that feigns calm,

Although it allows spinsters to enjoy a sweet old age

And can walk in silence even when not on a carpet;

The wolf, although a she-wolf had famous dugs;

The he-goat, although his skin furnishes humans with water bottles;

Despite the high price currently demanded for his skin, the otter;

Although his name designates a fabric, the alpaca.

Footnote 1 (from previous page), line 19 *d'illustres pis*: ie. the she-wolf that suckled Romulus and Remus.

84   *unanime*: cf. the penultimate paragraph of "Comment j'ai écrit certains de mes livres": "*Je ne connus vraiment la sensation du succès que lorsque je chantais en m'accompagnant au piano et surtout par de nombreuses imitations que je faisais d'acteurs ou de personnes quelconques. Mais là, du moins, le succès était énorme et unanime*" ("The only kind of success I have ever really experienced was while performing songs to my own piano accompaniments, and above all from my numerous impersonations of actors and a variety of ordinary people. But there at least my success was enormous and unanimous"; *CJ*, pp. 34–35).

86   *Balthazar*: Daniel 5.

90   *cheveu par cheveu*: Roussel grew obsessed as he approached fifty with the state of his own hair, and therefore, as Michel Leiris recounts, sought professional guidance: "on the advice of a respected doctor, he would, twice a week, heat each part of his hair with a hot-air dryer, until he could feel his hair almost burning. Remarking that, if he missed a single application, he would have to abandon the entire treatment, having broken the 'series,' he found himself forced, while travelling in regions where he could not use the appliance, which he'd always carry with him, to make use of pre-heated saucepans; on one occasion, unable to get hold of a saucepan, he used a sheet of hot metal, under which he had to kneel" (*RC*, p. 212).

Instruction *Mane Thecel Phares*: Numbered, weighed, divided.

A plain wall on which the words "*Mane Thecel Phares*" are written as if in letters of flame. Nothing else, no people, no feast. Lettering of the period. (lines 86–88)

Par l'action du temps, sa tête se déleste;))))
Se fait aux profondeurs du grand vide céleste
Où la lumière court sans jamais le franchir;
L'aphone à son ardoise, ennuyeuse à blanchir;)))
Il ne sait aux gifleurs que tendre l'autre joue,   95
Soit de ses fins talents s'il triche lorsqu'il joue;))
Sur celui qui s'éloigne on fait courir maints bruits;),
D'opaque frondaison, de rayons et de fruits.

By the mere action of time, the head is slowly unburdened;))))
Gets used to the depths of the vast heavenly void
Where light runs without ever exceeding its limits;
The mute gets used to his slate that is so wearisome to whiten;)))
He knows only how to turn the other cheek to those who slap him,
Or of his astute talents if he cheats at cards;))
About whoever is departing numerous rumors are started;),
With thick foliage, with glinting lights and fruits.

92   *Se fait aux profondeurs*: This returns us to the astronomer of line 24.

95   *Il ne sait*: This completes the syntactic unit interrupted at line 9.

97   *Sur celui qui s'éloigne*: The rumors started concern the elegant guest turning on his heels and leaving in line 4, and featured in the first illustration of the canto, no. 49.

A section of starry sky without any earthly landscape as if seen from some vantage point in space and giving the impression of infinity. (lines 92–93)